POETRY IS DEAD II
Once You're Dead, You're Dead Forever

D.L. Lang, Editor

©2025 Hercules Publishing

ISBN 979-8-218-54778-3

Hercules Publishing
Albuquerque, NM 87108
This anthology, © 2025 Hercules Publishing
Cover image: Oracle Park, San Francisco, CA
Dead & Company, July 16, 2023- PW Covington

Line edits by Leann Hurst Covington, PW Covington
1st revision 2/25

ISBN 979-8-218-54778-3

Designed/Produced in the United States of America

All rights reserved. No portion of this book may be reproduced in any form without permission from the publisher, except for brief passages for promotional or educational purposes and as otherwise permitted by U.S. copyright law. For permissions, contact individual contributors who hold and reserve all rights to their work.

POETRY IS DEAD II

Once You're Dead,
You're Dead Forever

D.L. Lang, Editor

HOW TO MAKE BREAKFAST OR WHATEVER WHILE FOLLOWING A TOUR ALL SUMMER BY JULEIGH HOWARD-HOBSON 1
THE GRATEFUL DEAD IS FAMILY BY HANNAH LIEBREICH 2
THE DAY EVERYTHING CHANGED BY K.LIPSCHUTZ.......................................3
DREAMSHIP BY BENGT O BJÖRKLUND 4
GARCIA IS WAITING 'TIL TOMORROW COMES BY JUDE BRIGLEY 5
RIPPLE ON THE ROAD BY CHANDER DHINGRA..6
TO STRING A CROWN OF SWEET SCARLET BEGONIAS UPON ME BY APRIL RIDGE...7
JUST ONE MORE SATURDAY NIGHT BY KAREN A VANDENBOS....................9
JUST DON'T CALL IT FRISCO BY JAY PASSER...10
THE QUESTION THAT KILLED CASSADY BY AIRLIFT UNDERGROUND 11
THERE IS A DOPPELGÄNGER PLANET BY TRISH HOPKINSON 15
A LONG STRANGE TRIP BY BARRIE PATTON 16
GRACELAND BY B. ELIZABETH BECK 18
ROLLING PAPERS, PIPES, BONGS, ROACH CLIPS BY RON WHITEHEAD 19
GRATEFUL DEAD, LSD & POETRY BROKE MY CHAIN BY CLAIRE CONROY 22
WHEN THEY WERE YOUNG BY CHRIS DEAN..23
GRATEFULLY BY MARK LIPMAN 24
DEADHEADS FROM JERSEY BY "CATFISH JOHN" WOJTOWICZ......................26
BLUES FOR A LONG STRANGE TRIP BY CHANDER DHINGRA 28
DREAMING WITH SAN FRANCISCO BY SUSAN BEALL SUMMERS 29
SAUSALITO GETAWAY BY OZ HARDWICK...30
TRAVELING TO THE DOCK OF THE BAY BY SUSAN BEALL SUMMERS 31
HAIGHT-ASHBURY REVERIE BY CHANDER DHINGRA.....................................32
AT THE TRUCK STOP, 1974 BY WILLIAM BUTLER 33
MY LIFE IN LYRICS BY ELIZABETH S. WOLF..34
YOU'RE CASEY JONES TONIGHT BY SUSAN BEALL SUMMERS......................35
SUGAR TAKES THE WHEEL BY SUSAN BEALL SUMMERS 36
DELIBERATELY LOST BY SUSAN BEALL SUMMERS 37
WHY I MISSED THE GRATEFUL DEAD CONCERT AT THE OAKLAND COLISEUM BY LENORE WEISS..38
COLISEUM LOT, 12/18/93 BY PAUL CORMAN-ROBERTS................................39
HIGHGATE VERMONT SUMMER TOUR JULY 1994 BY ELIZABETH S. WOLF ..42
GRATEFUL BY ANN SANCHEZ 43
FIRST TIME DEAD BY BECKY BISHOP WHITE 44

THE FIRST SHOW: JULY 4TH, 1990 BY DON MCIVER 46
ODE TO THE DEAD BY ROARSHOCK..49
MY BROTHER, WHO I ONLY SEE AT DEAD SHOWS BY PW COVINGTON 51
TRANSFORMATION INVITATION BY RENEE CHANDLER 53
SWEET DEAD HAIKUS BY CHUCK TAYLOR...55
STONED BY KEN GOODMAN 56
HIGH IDENTITY BY KEN GOODMAN...56
PSILOCYBIC SEXUAL MICROGRAVITY BY NANCY PATRICE DAVENPORT........57
TO THE MEN I MET AT A DEAD SHOW IN 1981 BY LEAH MUELLER 58
ALMOST FOUR P.M. BY B. ELIZABETH BECK 60
AURORA BOREALIS LADY BY NANCY PATRICE DAVENPORT..........................63
SET ON THE DEAD BY JIM LANDWEHR 64
NEVER MISS A SUNDAY SHOW BY J. MARTIN STRANGEWEATHER 66
DEAD POEM BY SCOT GRESHAM-LANCASTER 68
GLEN FALLS, '79 BY MARGARET R SÁRACO 69
FULL MOON ON HAMPTON BEACH BY TOMMY TWILITE..............................70
GRATEFUL: DEAD OR ALIVE BY JOE KIDD 71
PORTRAIT OF A DESERT CONCERT BY JON LAWRENCE 72
DANCE (DEAD SHOW) BY TRISH HOPKINSON...73
THE NIGHT I HEARD A NEW DEAD SONG BY ECKHARD GERDES 74
THAT WILL CHANGE TODAY BY ROLANDO SERNA 75
DEADHEADS : AN ERASURE POEM BY SUSAN BEALL SUMMERS..................77
UN-DEAD BY SUSAN BEALL SUMMERS...78
RADIO SAINTS BY DOUG D'ELIA 79
AFTER LISTENING TO GRATEFUL DEAD SONGS AT 4 AM BY JOHANNA ELY .80
SUSPENSION BY B. ELIZABETH BECK 81
WALK OUT OF ANY DOORWAY BY NANCY SOBANIK..................................... 83
PHONE CALL FROM MY NEPHEW BY ROBERT COOPERMAN 84
THE BASEBALL CAP BY ROBERT COOPERMAN...85
VISITING FRIENDS IN ATHENS, GEORGIA BY ROBERT COOPERMAN 86
SECOND VISIT TO THE AUDIOLOGIST'S OFFICE BY ROBERT COOPERMAN...87
BLUE PYRAMID BY ROARSHOCK..89
GRATEFUL KU BY JOHN SAVOIE..90
EVERY DAY BY PATRICIA J. DORANTES 92
A SWEET STAB TO MY HEART BY MOORE NGWENYA......................................93
GUITAR LESSONS BY UZOMAH UGWU 96
THE CROWD BY UZOMAH UGWU 97

I HAVE LIVED BY UZOMAH UGWU	98
FROM ITS LIFE— IT'S SOULE— IT'S BREATH! BY KATRENIA GRACE BUSCH	99
SING A SONG O YESTERDAY! BY KATRENIA GRACE BUSCH	100
FARE THEE WELL BY LYNN WHITE	101
MARRYING A DEADHEAD BY LISA SCHNAIDT	102
GONE BY B. ELIZABETH BECK	103
AT MY FUNERAL BY ECKHARD GERDES	104
BOB THOMAS BY HAKIM	105
CATS UNDER THE STARS BY SHANNON EDDY	106
GONE FOR GOOD BY HOWARD BROWN	108
RUMORS OF THE ANCIENT BY RENEE CHANDLER	109
(JUST) A BOX OF RAIN BY KEN GOODMAN	110
SUNDAY DAYDREAM BY D.L. LANG	111
WE HAD OUR PHIL BY ECKHARD GERDES	112
ASYMPTOTE BY SCOT GRESHAM-LANCASTER	113
THE GHOST SHIP ON THE BAY BY OZ HARDWICK	115
PHIL'S DEATH BY ROARSHOCK	116
OCEAN IN THE SKY BY BRUCE FISHER	118
ECHOES OF PHIL BY CHANDER DHINGRA	123
LESH PLAYS THE BASS LINE BY JUDE BRIGLEY	124
I THOUGHT OF YOU AT SUNRISE BY RENEE CHANDLER	125
IN MEMORY OF PHIL LESH BY ROBERT COOPERMAN	127
THE ROCK STAR FALLS IN GREATNESS BY MOORE NGWENYA	128
WITH REGARDS BY UZOMAH UGWU	129
DEEP, LIKE AN EARTHQUAKE BY PATRICIA J. DORANTES	130
LEARNING TO LIVE WITHOUT YOU BY JON LAWRENCE	131
DEAD HEAD ELEGY BY JIM MURPHY	132
AMERICAN ELEGY BY KYMBA NIJUCK	133
THE SECOND GIFT BY WENDY CARTWRIGHT	135
GARCIA'S DEATH BY ROARSHOCK	136
WHAT HAVE THE DEAD MEANT TO YOU? BY DAN O'CONNELL	139
TRANSFERRED BY M.D. DUNN	140
JERRY GARCIA DONE GONE LONG GONE BY BILL NEVINS	141
THE DAY CAPTAIN TRIPS DIED BY M.J. ARCANGELINI	143
UNCLE JERRY IN OHIO BY HEIDI JOFFE	145
JERRY GARCIA & GERMAN ROOT BEER BY JOHN DORSEY	146
DEAR JERRY BY MIKE FOXHALL	147

PIGPEN BY RENEE CHANDLER..149
POETRY IS DEAD BY CORBIN BUFF 150
HOME WITH THE GRATEFUL DEAD BY CHUCK TAYLOR................................152
THE ANSWER IS BY KEN GOODMAN..153
BLISS BLISS BLISS BY KEN GOODMAN..153
LOOK NO FURTHER BY KEN GOODMAN 154
UNCLE JOHN'S BAND BY JUDE BRIGLEY 155
A DREAM WE DREAMED SO LONG AGO BY KEITH FELTON.........................156
RIPPLE BY PESACH ROTEM 157
RIPPLIN' FOUNTAIN OF YOUTH BY RAYMOND SEWELL 158
[MY SON AND I SEARCHED FOR] BY DAVID RASKIN 159
SONGENIZIO ON A LINE FROM "BIRD SONG" BY ANDREW JONES.............160
TAKING THE T-SHIRT BY KENDALL SNEE 161
CASEY JONES BY KAREN CLINE-TARDIFF..164
GRATEFUL YOU'RE DEAD BY MADISON GILL-SILVA....................................165
TRUE TO ME, TRUE TO MY DYING DAY BY PEGGY BRENNAN 168
SATURDAY MORNING AA MEETING AT SAINT BEDE'S CHURCH BY NANCY PATRICE DAVENPORT 169
FLYING WITH THE DEAD BY DOUG D'ELIA..170
DOO DAH DOO DAH BY DAVID ALEC KNIGHT 174
DIRE WOLVES BY DAVID ALEC KNIGHT..175
THIS POEM IS WRITTEN IN BLOOD BY NANCY PATRICE DAVENPORT 176
WORD ART BY MIKE FERGUSON 178
QUENTIN TARANTINO LOVES THE GRATEFUL DEAD BY TRISH HOPKINSON 179

DEADicated to

Philip Chapman Lesh
(March 15, 1940 – October 25, 2024)

Bill Walton
(November 5, 1952 – May 27, 2024)

Fare thee well!
And if forever,
still forever,
fare thee well...

Lord Byron

FOREWORD

Poetry is Dead II: Once You're Dead, You're Dead Forever speaks to the way music can permeate our entire existence. The poets profess their love for a band whose music has become a soundtrack for milestones. The poems elevate mundane moments of daily life into a thing of beauty. This love is as timeless and all encompassing as the music itself, extending beyond lineup changes, band members' passing, and all geographical boundaries between fans.

In this anthology, a global cadre of deadhead poets send us on spiritual, musical, and psychedelic quests. Deadheads from around the world are included in these pages whether they fell in love with a few albums or dedicated their life to being die-hard loyal fans, trekking across the country in a nomadic musical pilgrimage, letting the experience transform them again and again. Poets from Canada, Mexico, Europe, Africa, and Asia as well as from over two dozen states in the United States are all included in these pages, reflecting a global fan community, showcasing the wide reach of the Dead's music.

They take us back to the 1960s, tripping across America and our minds. B. Elizabeth Beck's "Graceland" speaks to the multi-generational appeal of mid-century music: "We were too young for Woodstock / but old enough to get on the bus."

It begins with a deep dive into the concentric circles of community with Juleigh Howard-Hobson's beautiful suggestion to "Share all that grooviness."

It weaves its way down the road with "The Question that Killed Neal Cassady," showcasing Air Lift Underground's artful rhyme. Jay Passer blends musical countercultures blending the Grateful Dead with the Dead Kennedys' punk in "Just don't Call it Frisco." William Butler even makes a pit stop near my hometown of Enid, Oklahoma, experiencing a roadside anointing: "the Dead on the 8 track is salvation."

Several poets romanticize concerts attended, missed, and miracled across the United States, yet the Dead's recorded music remains with us even at 4 AM as Johanna Ely communes with angelic voices who visit in the twilight, asking "Are you kind?" The melodies accompany Rolando Serna while fishing and traversing the flea market, where "The bears / let you know: / "Yes, I am kind. / I know you are too."

Serna also asks, "I often wonder are there certain requirements to be, to become, to remain a deadhead?" This anthology does not gate keep. The poets herein reflect a broad community. Even if the poet themselves may question if they are qualified enough to be labelled a deadhead, they are welcome in these pages because it is the love of the music that connects us all no matter how, when, where or in what format we first became familiar with it.

The poetry in this book transcends reality, learning all there is to be learned from altered states both good and bad, transcribing it for those who remain on this plane. Bruce Fisher takes us past the "gelatinous membrane" to commune with migrating sea creatures and Phil Lesh.

The poems also speak frankly about the pitfalls of substances. Poets like Peggy Brennan celebrate achieving sobriety and finding strength in gratitude while Madison Gill-Silva mourns her late deadhead cousin who struggled with addiction. This dichotomy speaks to the broad spectrum of fans who enjoy the Dead's catalog of songs with or without chemical enhancement.

"Grateful" by Ann Sanchez describes the hypnotic multimedia experience of Dead & Company at the Las Vegas Sphere to "an interactive art display / that gave one euphoria without the high. / Like the cat that tries to chase the red dot, / you can not look at one place for too long."

Ekphrastic poems sparked by songs abound, including "Box of Rain," "Casey Jones," "Truckin'," "Ripple," and more. Poets such as Karen A VandenBos skillfully put song titles in a blender, assembling a musical mosaic of poetic narrative in "Just One More Saturday Night." In "A Long Strange Trip" Barrie Patton weaves a tale as wild as the Wizard of Oz, remixing song titles into a journey of discovery.

The writers herein romanticize their concert experiences and moments spent in deadhead community. Leah Mueller writes an ode "To the Men I Met at a Dead Show in 1981" where "thousands of freaks in sweaty tie-dyed / shirts, swirling and hugging, waving / our arms like trees in a windstorm."

While this anthology was mistaken by those who do not know the band as a general call for wrestling with mortality and the afterlife, and I had to correct assumptions and reject such poetry, there are a great number of elegies herein for Pigpen, Jerry Garcia, Phil Lesh, Bob Thomas, and tributes to those who turned them onto the band but are no longer on this earth.

Some speak of the music alone as a gateway to deep, spiritual experiences. In "Dear Jerry" Mike Foxhall reflects on finding serenity and divinity at the Sphere: "Being completely present in the moment, enjoying this music that has influenced, guided, and quite literally healed me, felt like I was touching the face of God. I have been to the mountain top. I have seen the white light. God is real, and God is love, and God is this music."

Poets speak to how the music comforted them in hard times and accompanied them through every stage of life, including as melodic midwifes into the afterlife. Eckhard Gerdes imagines how the Dead's music will play at his funeral, "Laugh and sing and drink till you fall, / and know that you're the poems / of my soul that I carry back whence I came." Robert Cooperman, rationally dismisses an afterlife, but still envisions Phil Lesh reuniting with his bandmates, "trading licks and riffs with Jerry / both of them in fine, fine form."

Trish Hopkinson takes us into a parallel universe where drug experimentation doesn't lead to addiction, rock stars achieve immortality beyond recording, and Pigpen's membership the 27 Club is rejected. Instead "Jimi, Janis, Jim & PigPen belt /on an open air stage / even as their necks / fold and crease, fingers curl, lips thin—hair catching white in starlight."

Many poems herein romanticize the 60s such as "When they were Young" by Chris Dean, who speaks of how culture is passed between the generations: "hippie children taught / a longing for going / knowing all the words /before they knew how to talk." Oz Hardwick's "Sausalito Getaway" imagines "Smiling skeletons line the road, / thumbs outstretched and beat guitar cases / slung across their frugging shoulders, /each clutching a sign that reads 'Furthur.'" Chander Dhingra's "Haight-Ashbury Reverie" marks the moment of collective transformation that "we became one with the music, / fading into the chords of eternity."

Others like Bill Nevins' "Jerry Garcia Done Long Gone" are more critical of that era's artistic legacy, speaking to the tension between old left and new left: "Woodstock was a mud n granola fiddle-fun fest while Indochina burned," and the gap between merely singing words of protest and bearing witness versus direct action, claiming, "Young Neil nor Joni never got gassed, shot or beat up / and no cop knocked the silver spoon / out of any Canadian folkie's dulcet mouth." The poem encourages a return to "dancing in the street" over being "on our own" as a solution to these rhyming times.

I have divided the text into sections based on content, starting with some psychedelia to set the scene, weaving in ekphrastic poems inspired by various songs, then concert reflections followed by some of the darker submissions that touch on heavier subjects like the tragic loss of band members or fellow deadheads, and the difficulties of seeking sobriety. In tweaking the book in some cases I was lenient about grammar, capitalization, and punctuation rules because some poets eschew them stylistically. In other cases, I found it necessary to edit.

I began compiling this anthology in July 2024. In the early months, wanting to get into the right headspace for such a project, I visited 710 Ashbury in San Francisco where the Grateful Dead lived in the 1960s. I got a contact high at Jerry Day at Jerry Garcia Amphitheater at McLaren Park. The venue rules said no substances, but the cops looked the other way at the plume of smoke lingering in the air.

I saw Phil Lesh & Friends play at Sunday Daydream in San Rafael, California on July 21st, 2024. Among the songs performed were "Jack Straw," "Scarlet Begonias," "Truckin'," "Sugar Magnolia," and "Somewhere over the Rainbow." My sole contribution is "Sunday Daydream" which reflects on this concert experience. A week out from the November 1st deadline, Phil passed away. I soon realized I had attended his last public performance.

The day after Phil passed, I returned to 710 Ashbury to leave some flowers at the front gate and at Phil's heart on the street beside Love on Haight. My husband and I wandered up to San Rafael and gazed up at the giant boat that once marked Terrapin Crossroads.

We peered through the wrought iron gate at 20 Front Street. Le Club Front is such a nondescript building in the canal district, you'd hardly have an inkling of the musical magic that once flowed where the Grateful Dead recorded their later albums.

As a testament to the community that has formed around this music, I asked the contributors to send me additional poems in honor of Phil Lesh. Those poems begin with "Rumors of the Ancient" by Renee Chandler and end with "Deep, Like an Earthquake" by Patricia J. Dorantes.

My love of the Grateful Dead's music started sometime in late 1997 when a documentary about the band was broadcast on VH-1, weaving together this mystical history where Mother McCree's Uptown Jug Champions were cast under the spell of the Warlocks until destiny wielded the synchronicity of the dictionary and dubbed them the Grateful Dead.

The television spoke of the glory of the beats, Greenwich village folkies and harmonious hootenannies, and the hippie scene in Haight Ashbury—a trip laced with love. Album art mysteries were decoded before my eyes with secret love notes for fans to unravel. This anthology is a good reflection of that whole scene.

American Beauty and *Workingman's Dead* became my steady musical companions whenever I mowed the lawn in the scorching Oklahoma heat as a teenager. Episode 18 of *Freaks & Geeks* further planted seeds in my teenaged mind. At 21 I finally set foot in the Haight after a Greyhound bus trip. Songs like "Truckin'" and "Casey Jones" journeyed with me down Route 66. Their harmonies sheltered my spirit like a guardian angel as I crossed the country with hundreds of wandering strangers.

Be Casey Jones be lauded as a hard-working railroad man, deemed a lousy scab by Seeger, or a workaholic fueled by coke, the characters of America's history and myth lives on in its folk, and the Dead are a solid link in that musical chain, reaching beyond their generation. At the end of the journey, may you emerge going down the road feeling good once again.

D.L. Lang

CONTRIBUTOR BIOS

Air Lift Underground is a word jazz/electronic hippie-hop duo practicing the Great Work in California. "The Question That Killed Cassady" appears on their first album, *No Mind Left Unblown* (nomindleft.com). Written by Amana Mission and Indi Riverflow.

M.J. Arcangelini, b.1952, has published extensively in magazines and anthologies. He has done an array of things to keep a roof over his head, some of them highly questionable but none of them too profitable. He is currently trying, unsuccessfully, to retire. He has 6 published collections, the most recent of which is *PAWNING MY SINS*, 2022 (Luchador Press).

B. Elizabeth Beck is a poet who writes fiction. *Dancing on the Page* (Rabbit House Press, 2024) is her fifth poetry collection. Accents Publishing will publish *Swan Songs*, her debut collection of short stories. She is the author of the *Summer Tour Trilogy*. Elizabeth is a recipient of The Kentucky Foundation for Women grant. Her work appears in journals and anthologies, including *Poetica Magazine, Appalachian Review, Limestone Blue*, and Harvard Education Press. Elizabeth founded two poetry series, Teen Howl, and Poetry at the/'tā-bəl/ in Lexington, Kentucky. For more information about Elizabeth: www.elizbeck.com

Becky Bishop White is a third-generation Californian who spent her formative years in NYC and Cambridge, MA. She returned West to attend UC Berkeley and acquired a BA with distinction in English. In recent years, her poems have earned awards and honorable mentions and have been selected for publication in various venues. She loves life with her husband, author James W. White, where they enjoy the arts and culture in the greater SF Bay Area as well as in the artsy waterside towns by the Carquinez Strait.

Bengt O Björklund was born in Stockholm 1949. Started to write poetry in a jail cell in Istanbul 1969. Sweden Beat Poet Laureate lifetime 2018. First listened to The Dead mid sixties as a hippie in Sweden dreaming of Haight-Ashbury.

PeggyO Brennan is a multimedia artist in the DC suburbs, mostly focusing on guitar. She attempted to make a *Grateful Dead Illustrated Lyrics* of deadhead artwork in 1987, but Hunter was simultaneously creating *Box of Rain*, so it was not to be. Peggy serves and benefits from Wharf Rats still for decades, and focuses deeply on spirituality. Peggy O has been performing folk rock since it was top forty! A multimedia artist from Washington DC, PeggyO lives in a tiny community with her dog and cat. www.bearhawk.world

Jude Brigley is Welsh. She has been a teacher, an editor and a performance poet. She now writes more for the page and has been published in various magazines. Her musical tastes were formed in the late 1960s and early 1970s and although it has expanded she is still loyal to her first loves.

Howard Brown is a retired attorney who lives on Lookout Mountain, TN with his wife, Ann, and wily cat, Stormy. His poetry has appeared in *Burningword Literary Journal, Printed Words, Blue Collar Review, Tuck Magazine, The Beautiful Space, Pure Slush, Truth Serum, Poetry Super Highway, Old Hickory Review, Devil's Party Press, Tiny Seed Literary Journal, Fleas on the Dog* and *Lone Stars Magazine*. He is the author of two collections of poetry, i.e. "The Gossamer Nature of Random Things" and "Variations in the Perception of Color." His poem "Pariah" won first place in the poetry division of the 2015 William Faulkner Literary Competition. His short fiction has appeared in *Louisiana Literature, F**k Fiction, Crack the Spine, Pulpwood Fiction, Extract(s), Gloom Cupboard, Full of Crow* and *Pure Slush*. His attraction to the Dead is longstanding, dating back to time living in Berkeley, California in the late 70's, hearing tales from friends who had seen them live and listening to their records. This attraction has now been passed on to his grandson, who has a Grateful Dead poster in his room at the University of Miami, where he is a freshman.

Corbin Buff is a freelance writer living in western Montana. The lyrics of the Grateful Dead (particularly those penned by Robert Hunter) were some of his earliest influences that made him want to become a writer. Corbin is also a guitarist, and the playing of Jerry Garcia has been an equally influential and life- changing inspiration, introducing him to whole new genres of music and taking him down many fun rabbit holes. *"So many roads, so many roads..."*

Katrenia Grace Busch is a freelance journalist whose work can be found amongst NPR affiliate radio stations and CBS affiliate TV stations. She holds an associate's degree in journalism and general studies. Her publications have appeared amongst *50 Give or Take, Flora Fiction, Whimsical Poet, Red Penguin Books, October Hill* among others. She is a poetry editor for Zoetic Press and *The Bookends Review* and serves on a local play reading committee. She also serves on an editorial board for the American Psychological Association and as a federal grant reviewer for the U.S. Department of Justice and is the author of the forthcoming poetry chapbook mini-series *"The Cardinal Chronicles"* with the inaugural book *Mystery and Wind* and its subsequent, *This Cardinal Book*. She has appeared as a guest on *Quintessential Listening*. She can be found on Facebook here: https://www.facebook.com/profile.php?id=100087528584176

William Butler has been writing and jiving in Memphis, TN., New Orleans, LA, and points in between since the 60's. A Dead Head preachin' the gospel of Forever in the Home of the Blues, the Birthplace of Rock 'N Roll, and the Home of the King of RnR, Elvis!

Wendy Cartwright is a poet/artist/author/reporter/columnist/weirdo out of Columbus, Indiana. Her travels have taken her as far as Mayan Ruins and as near as the filling station. Her undiscerning tastes allow her to find creative fodder regardless of location. She has been published in various print anthologies and been featured in online publications. She has self-published three books and has another manuscript in the works.

Renee Chandler was born in Providence, Rhode Island and now lives in Massachusetts with her 12-year-old-daughter. She got turned onto the Dead in her early 20's and since then has allowed their music to slowly seep into her bones. Today, going to as many shows and iterations of their music as possible is at the forefront of defining her passion. She has pursued her love of writing through tutoring and aiding others in their adventures through higher education. Renee is an advocate of mental wellness and a cheerleader for artists in every realm, providing unwavering support and respect to others on their healing journeys.

Emecheta Christian is a brilliant writer whose work explores themes of self-actualization, belonging, and the complexities of the human experience. His works have appeared in esteemed literary journals and anthologies such as *The Potter's Poetry, Indiana Review, Oxford American, Four Way Review, the Academy of American Poets Poem-A-Day Series*, and elsewhere. He has been recognized with several awards, including the Iroko Award and The Dorothy Hewett Award. Emecheta's unique voice and evocative imagery have garnered him a growing reputation as a voice of change in the global literary scene.

Karen Cline-Tardiff has been writing as long as she could hold a pen. Her works have appeared in several anthologies and journals, both online and in print. She stays up too late and snoozes her alarm past any reasonable time. She is founder and Editor-in-Chief of Gnashing Teeth Publishing. Find her at karenthepoet.com

Beat Poet Laureate of Maine 2024-2026, **Claire Conroy** has self published two books of poetry ("Listen" in 2018 and "Silent" in 2022) and a chapbook ("Rumors From Dead Lips" in 2024). Born in Portsmouth, NH, she is a proud board member of the Portsmouth Poet Laureate Program and is the host of their open mic, The HOOT. She has had over a dozen anthologies and has been translated into Hindi by Devesh Path Sariya. Claire lives in Sanford, Maine.

Robert Cooperman is the author of over twenty poetry collections, five of which were inspired by the Grateful Dead. In addition, *In the Colorado Gold Fever Mountains* won the Colorado Book Award for Poetry for 2000. *Draft Board Blues* was named one of Ten Great Reads for 2017 by a Colorado Author, by *Westword Magazine*. *Youth's Joyful Noise*, Cooperman's latest tribute to the Grateful Dead, was published in 2023 by Kelsay Books.

Paul Corman-Roberts is the author of the Firecracker nominated poetry collection *Bone Moon Palace* (Black Lawrence Press, 2021) the graphic chapbook *The Sincere* (Libran Apocalypse, 2022) and the forthcoming *19th Street Station Volume 2* (Collapse Press.) He's a free range educator for hire and is getting back into playing percussion.

PW Covington is the National Beat Poetry Foundation's 2024 2026 "New Mexico Beat Poet Laureate," and founder of Hercules Publishing. His first Dead show was Mountain View 1993, which he attended while assigned to temporary duty at Travis Air Force Base in California. Find and friend him on Facebook.

Nancy Patrice Davenport is a native of the San Francisco Bay Area. She lives in Menlo Park with three cats. Nancy has been writing since 2012. Her poems have been published in journals and anthologies, and have been translated into several languages. Nancy had a poem nominated for 2016 Best of Net. Nancy's first book, *LA BRIZNA*, was published in 2014 by Bookgirl Press; her second, *SMOKING IN MOM'S GARAGE* was published in 2018 by Red Alice Press, her third collection, *NOTHING AND TOO*

MUCH TO TALK ABOUT, was published in 2023 by Roadside Press. She's currently working on her fourth collection.

Doug D'Elia, poet, novelist, playwright, photographer, and visual artist, was born in Holyoke, Massachusetts. He served as a medic during the Vietnam War and earned his B.A. in Philosophy and Religion from the University of Central Florida. His poetry and short stories appear in over 50 publications domestically and internationally, and his haiku has been translated and published in English and Mandarin. He is the author of two novellas, three collections of poetry, one book of short stories, and two books of poetography (poems and photographs). Three of his plays have been performed at theatres in Tallahassee, Houston, and Syracuse. His first Grateful Dead show was in 1968 at the Fillmore East in NYC. Doug currently divides his time between Brooklyn, New York, and Syracuse, New York.

Chris Dean is a storyteller, spoken word artist and self-proclaimed Magpie Poet who writes from the heart of Indiana where they live with their husband, dog and too many cats to mention. Their work has been featured online, in multiple print anthologies and they are the author of two books of poetry, *Tales From a Broken Girl* and *We're All Stories in the End*, published by Storeylines Press.

Chander Dhingra is a 3D artist and writer with a passion for storytelling. His work explores themes of personal transformation and the human condition. He has extensive experience in 3D environment design and teaching digital tools, and is also fascinated by Indian mythology and Sigma male psychology.

Born and raised in Mexico City, **Patricia J. Dorantes** has been a lover of anything creativity-related since she was quite young. This natural curiosity Left her to have knowledge on the psychology and marketing fields. Growing up surrounded by fans of psychedelic music, is only natural that a love for that kind of sounds began growing inside her, which lead her to take a couple of rock-history-related college-level courses, where she discovered the Dead, and almost instantly feel in love with the unique aesthetic and original sound of the band.

John Dorsey is the former Poet Laureate of Belle, MO. He is the author of several collections of poetry, including *Which Way to the River: Selected Poems: 2016-2020* (OAC Books, 2020), *Sundown at the Redneck Carnival*, (Spartan Press, 2022) and *Pocatello Wildflower*, (Crisis Chronicles Press, 2023).

Musician and writer **M.D. Dunn** has published three books of poetry and nine albums. His most recent nonfiction book is the IPPY-award winning bestseller: *You Get Bigger as You Go: Bruce Cockburn's Influence and Evolution*, a beginner's guide to the great Canadian songwriter. Find him online at www.mddunn.com

Shannon Eddy is a New England poet. Studied at URI, volunteer and post grad with OSSTIC. Published in *Naugatuck River Review* and *Chaparral*. He also goes by @angrypoetri on social media running The Three Words Project.

Johanna Ely served as the sixth poet laureate of Benicia, California from 2016-2018. Her most recent poetry collection is Titled, *What Still Matters* (Last Laugh Productions 2023). She has also co-authored a book with three other women poets Titled, *Love's Meditation* (Random Lane Press 2023). Listening to "American Beauty" always makes her feel nostalgic for my misspent youth.

Keith Felton was born in Pittsburgh, Pennsylvania. He received a degree in English Literature from Duquesne University. For many years he divided his time between San Francisco and Berlin Germany, but now resides full time in San Francisco. He has been a featured reader at poetry readings at The Beat Museum, The Caffe Trieste, The Savoy Tivoli, Le Petit Paris 75, The Cafe Greco, Bird and Beckett Books, First Fridays North Beach, and The San Francisco Presidio Branch Library. His poetry has been anthologized, and his small edition chapbook poem, *A Literary History of San Francisco* was published by Off The Cuff Press.

Mike Ferguson is an American permanently resident in the UK. His most recent poetry collection is *the aran aphorisms* (Red Ceilings Press, 2024).

Bruce Fisher is a poet living in San Francisco. He heard "Playing in the Band" on the *Skull and Roses* album in the late seventies and that changed everything.

Mike Foxhall is a realtor and Dead Head living in Birmingham, AL. He's the father of two boys that he thoroughly enjoys introducing The Dead to, and loves nothing more than bringing new people to this community. He is both thrilled and honored to be part of this project.

Eckhard Gerdes "At My Funeral" is from the anthology and accompanying CD *Blues for Youse* (ATTOHO, 2014). The poem is about something's been asking his kids to do for years, which is to play

"He's Dead" at his funeral and to dance in a conga line for it. He wants people to have fun at his funeral and to remember his joy, not his suffering. He has stories that he will have to tell someday if he ever gets around to an autobiography. He keep himself too busy writing my novels, usually, but occasionally forays into poetry (He have published two collections, including *Blues for Youse*), drama, and creative nonfiction, including *How to Read* which has generated a very positive response.

Madison Gill-Silva is an award-winning poet from Colorado and author of *Casualties of Honey* (Middle Creek Publishing 2023) whose work has appeared in a variety of print and online publications. She lives with her husband and their cat in a tiny house on Colorado's western slope. Her connection to the Grateful Dead is through her late cousin, John Ryan Stinar, who was a bonafide Dead Head. Now whenever "Brokedown Palace" plays during a shuffle of her 2,000 liked songs on Spotify, or she sees a Stealie sticker on the napkin dispenser at her table in some nowhere-town bar – she smiles and looks to the sky, sensing his spirit is near.

Joe Kidd is a working, poet/songwriter/artist. In 2020, published The Invisible Waterhole, a collection of spiritual and sensual verse. Awarded by the Michigan Governor's Office and the United States House of Representatives. Joe was Beat Poet Laureate State of Michigan 2022-2024, and Official Poet of the Government of Birland North Africa. He holds an Honorary Doctorate from International Union Peace Federation. With Sheila Burke he has toured Europe, North America, & Caribbean Islands. He has been featured in international anthologies, magazines, websites, festivals, and other personal appearances. Joe is a member of National & International Beat Poet Foundation, 100 Thousand Poets For Change, Society of Classical Poets, and Michigan Rock & Roll Hall Of Fame. Official Website: www.joekiddandsheilaburke.com

Scot Gresham-Lancaster, born in 1954 in Redwood City, California, is an American composer, performer, instrument builder, and educator known for his pioneering work in computer network music. He doesn't identify as a poet, but if asked to, he would play one on television. He is a member of The Hub, a group that explores the interaction between performers and computers through interconnected music machines.

Hannah Liebreich grew up in a household filled with music. As a child, her mom played piano, and her dad would sing and play the Grateful Dead and Bob Dylan on the guitar. As an academic Hannah has had to move to different parts of the country for work and finds joy, comfort, and community seeing Grateful Dead cover bands wherever she lives. When she's not at local shows or spending time with family, you'll find Hannah on the road with the Cincy Trash Crew seeing Goose, Billy Strings, and other up and coming jam bands.

K.Lipschutz (formerly klipschutz) is the author of *Mr. Congeniality* (2021) and seven other collections, starting with *The Erection of Scaffolding for the Re-Painting of Heaven by the Lowest Bidder* (1985). He has also co-written over a hundred songs released by international recording artist Chuck Prophet. *Long Engagement: New & Selected Poems (1985–2023)*, assembled in conjunction with long-Time supporter Brenda Hillman, is looking for a home. He lives in downtown San Francisco with Colette Jappy and two cats.

Ken Goodman's Dark Star crashes, pouring its light into ashes in Cleveland, Ohio.

Hakim, long a mainstay of both Los Angeles and Orange Counties, returns to the scene after an absence of several years. During extended stays in Mexico, Istanbul, Costa Rica, Italy and Greece, he studied the ancient Persian romance tradition & early 20th-century surrealists - and now the one-Time Southern California street poet & frequent Slam winner lives in Northern California. Hakim's most recent book, *Posed Perfectly in Dreams*, was published by Prometheus Press.

Oz Hardwick is an award-winning poet, photographer, occasional musician, and accidental academic, whose work has been widely published in international journals and anthologies. He has published "a dozen or so" full collections and chapbooks, most recently *Retrofuturism for the Dispossessed* (Hedgehog, 2024). His manuscript *Orion Highway* won the 2024 Dolors Alberola International Poetry Prize and will be published by Dalya Press in 2025. Oz has held residencies in the UK, Europe, the US, and Australia, and has performed internationally at major festivals and in tiny coffee shops. Buying 1972's *Glastonbury Fayre* triple album for the unreleased Hawkwind tracks, Oz first encountered the Dead through the 25-minute extract of 'Dark Star' thereon. Subsequently, it's been a long, strange trip indeed, and although he only got to see the band live a couple of times, the recordings have made up a considerable part of the soundtrack to the intervening half century or so. Oz is Professor of Creative Writing at Leeds Trinity University.

Trish Hopkinson is a poet and advocate for the literary arts. You can find her online at SelfishPoet.com and in western Colorado where she runs the regional poetry group Rock Canyon Poets and is a board member of the International Women's Writing Guild. Her poetry has been published in *Sugar House*

Review, TAB: The Journal of Poetry & Poetics, and The Penn Review; and her most recent book A Godless Ascends was published by Lithic Press in March 2024. Hopkinson happily answers to labels such as atheist, feminist, and empty nester; and enjoys traveling, live music, and craft beer.

Juleigh Howard-Hobson's work can be found in Able Muse, Think Journal, The Buddhist Review, Autumn Sky Poetry, Great Weather for Media, Under Her Skin (Black Spot Books), Weaving the Terrain: 100-word Southwest Poems (Dos Gatos Press) and many other venues. She has been nominated for "The Best of the Net", the Pushcart, the Elgin and the Rhysling Awards. Her latest collection is Curses, Black Spells and Hexes (Alien Buddha Press). She spent nearly a decade dropped out, living off-grid in a converted school bus that had a print of the SYF skull stuck up where the rearview mirror used to be. This poem is dedicated to the friend who first introduced her to the music and the vibe, long long ago. X: @poetforest

Heidi Joffe (M.Ed.) is a published poet and multimedia artist who crafts meaning with fibers, clay, and words.

Andrew Jones lives in Iowa and teaches at the University of Dubuque. He is the author of Liner Notes (Kelsey Books, 2020) and his writing has appeared in publications such as North American Review, Sierra Nevada Review, and Split Rock Review, as well as the anthology Visiting Bob: Poems Inspired by the Life and Work of Bob Dylan (New Rivers Press, 2018). Though the music was always adjacent to his life, it took him many years to embrace the Dead fully. Now he shares frequent morning spins of Blues for Allah with his 15-year-old daughter.

David Alec Knight grew up in Chatham, Ontario, Canada. He was recipient of the Ted Plantos Memorial Award for Poetry, 2021. Recent work has appeared in Verse Afire, Night Owl Narrative, Tickets To Midnight Volume 2 - It's Human, Starman Oddity Anthology - Poetry And Art Inspired By David Bowie, and Stormwash: Environmental Poems. His most recent book, Leper Mosh (Cajun Mutt Press, 2022), is his first book to feature his own art on the cover. Other artistic interests include abstract painting with acrylics. As for his interest in the Grateful Dead, it all started way back when he was a kid and there was one babysitter who would play Terrapin Station when she was over.

Jim Landwehr has six poetry collections, Tea in the Pacific Northwest, Thoughts from a Line at the DMV, Genetically Speaking, On a Road, Reciting from Memory, and Written Life. Jim also has four published memoirs, At the Lake, Cretin Boy, Dirty Shirt and The Portland House. He is retired and lives with his wife in Waukesha, Wisconsin. **Web:** jimlandwehr.com

Jon Lawrence currently teaches high school English and Creative Writing in his hometown of Bethlehem, Pennsylvania. He received an MFA in Creative Writing at the Maslow Family Graduate Program in Creative Writing at Wilkes University. He is the author of the chapbook A Phrase Which Becomes Us (Bottlecap Press, 2024), and his poetry and reviews have been published in Newfound, American Writers Review, The Bangalore Review, Wild Roof Journal, and others.

Mark Lipman, US National Beat Poet Laureate 2024-2025; founder of the press Vagabond, the Culver City Book Festival, and the Elba Poetry Festival; winner of the 2015 Joe Hill Labor Poetry Award; the 2016 International Latino Book Award and the 2023 L'Alloro di Dante (Dante's Laurel – Ravenna, Italy), a writer, poet, multi-media artist, activist and author of fifteen books, began his career as the writer-in residence at the world famous Shakespeare and Company in Paris, France (2002-2003). Since then he has worked closely with such legendary poets as Lawrence Ferlinghetti and Jack Hirschman on many projects, and for the last twenty years has established a strong international following as a leading voice of his generation. He's the host and foreign correspondent for the radio program, Poetry from Around the World, for Poets Café on KPFK 90.7FM Los Angeles. As Mark continues to travel the world, he uses poetry to connect communities to the greater social justice issues, while building consciousness through the spoken word.

Don McIver is a poet, DJ, writer, Deadhead living in Albuquerque, NM. He marks the day he attended his first Dead show as the most formative event he's had as an adult.

Leah Mueller has enjoyed the Grateful Dead for over forty years, though she only saw them in concert five times. Her favorite Dead album is Europe '72. Leah's work appears in Rattle, NonBinary Review, Brilliant Flash Fiction, Citron Review, The Spectacle, New Flash Fiction Review, Atticus Review, Your Impossible Voice, etc. She has been nominated for Pushcart and Best of the Net. Leah appears in the 2022 edition of Best Small Fictions. Her fourteenth book, Stealing Buddha was published by Anxiety Press in 2024. Website: www.leahmueller.org.

Ted Mc Carthy is a poet, translator and playwright living in Clones, Ireland. His work has appeared in magazines in Ireland, the UK, Germany, the USA, Canada and Australia. He has had two collections published, *November Wedding*, and *Beverly Downs*. His work can be found on www.tedmccarthyspoetry.weebly.com

Jim Murphy is the author of four poetry collections: *Versions of May*, *The Uniform House*, *Heaven Overland*, and *The Memphis Sun*. His poems and scholarship have appeared in journals including *Brooklyn Review, Gulf Coast, MELUS, Mississippi Review, Modern Fiction Studies, Puerto del Sol, The Southern Review, Texas Review* and *TriQuarterly*. He teaches at the University of Montevallo and lives with his family in Birmingham, Alabama.

Bill Nevins, born August 4, 1947 is a poet, a songwriter, a journalist and a retired University of New Mexico educator who has worked in various media including film and video. Bill grew up in the US northeast and he has lived in New Mexico since 1996. Bill graduated from Iona College, did graduate work in literature at U. of Connecticut and U. California at Berkeley and visited Ireland, Spain, Mexico, NYC, New Orleans and other places during both troubled and happier times. He is a father and grandfather. His collection, *Light Bending*, will be published by Sligo Creek Publishing.

Moore Ngwenya is a Swazi poet residing in the Kingdom of Eswatini who writes a variety of poems including Christian poetry, inspirational poems and various poems about national or worldwide celebrated events, and is working on compiling a debut poetry collection.

Kymba Nijuck paints, writes, films, makes tarot decks, & works with dreams & for social justice. Her art has been shown in galleries, museums, and film festivals on 3 continents.

Dan O'Connell is a four-Time award winning poet, and multiple finalist and honorable mention. Although not a Dead Head, he has been to many Dead-related shows with Dead Head friends, and was struck by what Jerry Garcia said, quoted in the poem. This poem is written from Jerry's perspective. (He was referencing Cary Grant who said: "We all wish we were Cary Grant. Sometimes I wish I was Cary Grant.")

Jay Passer's poetry first appeared in *Caliban* magazine, alongside the work of William S. Burroughs, Maxine Hong Kingston, and Wanda Coleman, in 1988. Subsequently, Passer's literary output has been included in numerous print and online publications, as well as several anthologies, including 2014's Friends of the San Francisco Public Library's Poets 11 issue, representing the Tenderloin District, selected and edited by San Francisco Poet Laureate Jack Hirschman. He is the author of 15 collections of poetry and prose, and a debut novel, *Squirrel*, was released in 2022. His work can be found in *Don't Submit!, The Rye Whiskey Review, The Gorko Gazette, Mad Swirl, Odd Magazine, Graffiti Kolkata, Red Fez, Otoliths, Beatnik Cowboy, Horror Sleaze Trash, Poetry Super Highway, Lothlorien Poetry Journal* and *Urban Pigs Press*. A lifetime plebeian, Passer has labored as dishwasher, soda jerk, barista, pizza cook, housepainter, courier, warehouseman, bookseller, and mortician's apprentice. His latest collection of poems, *Son of Alcatraz*, released by Alien Buddha Press in February 2024, is available from Amazon. Originally a native of San Francisco, he currently resides in Los Angeles, with a legion of imaginary cats and some very real houseplants.

Barrie Patton has been on that proverbial bus for over 40 years. In the early 80's around the age of 14, I met my first husband, who introduced me to the Grateful Dead. The first song I ever really heard was "Wharf Rat," and it will hold a special place forever. He took me to my first show, which was Jerry Garcia Band with Melvin Seals. It was there that I jumped on the bus so fast! After that we ran to every show we could, along with my sister, and so many friends! The energy of the shows, the feeling you would get just being surrounded by the music and the people have always been incredible. From getting the tickets to the drive there, to the lot, the show and the walk back to the car, it was like being in a totally different world. It was never "just music," but an experience and lifestyle. Life happened, we had 3 kids, divorced, got remarried, have 2 perfect grandbabies now. And thankfully all are lovers of the music and experience. I'll forever be grateful for this long strange trip it's been.

David Raskin sang Grateful Dead songs at Camp Timberlane in Northern Wisconsin during the '70s and '80s: "Dire Wolf," "Ripple," and, at every campfire, "The Doctor Song." He teaches ekphrasis and art history at the School of the Art Institute of Chicago and has participated in the Bread Loaf Writers' Conference and three *Kenyon Review* Writers Workshops. See more at www.davidraskin.com.

April Ridge scrawls messages in the night on the clouds that dreams are made of. She whispers sweet nothings to the muses of time and revels in the chance to swim in the deep nothingness of silence, if only to shout 'Echo' in it. She has enjoyed the Grateful Dead since young adolescent meanderings brought her to the album *American Beauty*, which she believes to be one of the Holy Grail 'perfect albums' that are whispered about in the sacred halls of music history. April prides herself on finding the perfect tie dyed outfit in which to adorn the rose-strewn skeleton of the soul. She hopes to highlight the needs of poems in danger, on the run, escaping from the need to fit into one form or another, on their way to the freedom of epiphany.

Pesach Rotem was born and raised in New York. He was blessed to have an older brother who turned him on to the novels of Kurt Vonnegut, the movies of the Marx Brothers, the paintings of Salvador Dali, and the music of the Grateful Dead. His favorite album is *American Beauty*. He now lives in Yodfat, Israel, with his wife Coco and a few cats. He is a member of the Voices Israel Group of Poets in English and the Israel Association of Writers in English, and he serves as barman at the Karmiel Folk Klub.

Ann Sanchez is a native of the Rio Grande Valley in Texas, residing in the Mission/Edinburg area. She is a graduate of the University of Texas-Rio Grande Valley with a Bachelors of Fine Arts-Art. She has been published in UTRGV's *Gallery Magazine, Rio Grande Valley International Poetry Festival Boundless Anthology, Hercules Press Nowhere Poetry and Flash Fiction,* and *Poetry is Dead: An Inclusive Anthology of Deadhead Poetry.*

John Savoie teaches great books, Homer to Hunter, at Southern Illinois University Edwardsville. His first poetry collection *Sehnsucht* has recently won the Prize Americana. The lyrics first drew me to the Grateful Dead, only then the jams. Centuries ago Alexander Pope observed: "The sound must seem an echo to the sense." So it is with the Dead at their best, to my own ears never done more sublimely than in the performance of "Row Jimmy" on March 20, 1977 at Winterland. Garcia's second solo explores a melancholy that turns progressively sweeter (not unlike the coda to "Layla") until sorrow and sweetness tumble forth as one. Emerging from the solo Garcia calmly sings, "Broken heart don't feel so bad / you ain't got half of what you thought you had," as if the lyrics captioned what the band had just played. Even closer than an echo, the sound is the sense; the sense is the sound.

Margaret R. Sáraco is the author of *If There is No Wind* and *Even the Dog Was Quiet* (Human Error Publishing). She was nominated for a Pushcart and received multiple recognitions in the Allen Ginsberg Poetry Contest. Margaret is a poetry editor for the *Platform Review*. https://margaretsaraco.com.

Lisa Schnaidt has been a devoted Deadhead for over 46 years, thanks to her beloved husband, John, who introduced her to the magic of the Grateful Dead. Our deep appreciation for the band's music was a constant source of joy and connection throughout their marriage. As a widow the music will evoke memories and soothe her soul. Two kids, 2 grandsons, our beloved dog, Bailey, a life full of love, music, and travel made for a life well-lived. #NFA

Rolando Serna is a United States Marine/Gulf War Veteran MOS 7222, who started writing while serving time in federal prison. He's been published in University of Texas Pan-American's *Panorama* and *Gallery* magazines, *La Bolga* online publication, *2023 Boundless the Anthology of the Rio Grande Valley International Poetry Festival,* and *Poetry is Dead an Inclusive Anthology of Grateful Dead Poetry.* He holds a bachelor's degree in English with a minor in Spanish, and Master of Arts in English and Mexican American Studies. He is a member of the Nueva Onda Poets, No Name Poetry Group, Novena Poetry Group, Write Stuff Writers Group, and a founding member of Sloth Tea, and Poetry. I am just an old guy who has lived an interesting life, loves the Grateful Dead, and is a father.

Raymond Sewell is a Mi'kmaw poet and professor from Canada. An avid songwriter, Raymond tours and performs poetry across North America.

Kendall Snee is a 10th grade English teacher and Pittsburgh poet. She is the current Writer-in-Residence for Pittsburgh's City Books and a board member for Write Pittsburgh. She has made a name for herself among the Carlow University Mad Women, with her work appearing in *Voices from the Attic, Dionne's Story* for sexual assault survivors, and Pittsburgh's *Yawp* magazine. Pre-pandemic, Snee won Pittsburgh's Nasty Slam spoken word poetry and now reads with the Pittsburgh Poetry Collective / Steel City Slam.

Nancy Sobanik is a poet whose work can be found upcoming in *Frost Meadow Review, Vol. 12,*

Triggerfish Critical Review; Sparks of Calliope- Best of The Net Nominee 2023 and Pushcart Nomination 2024; *Verse-Virtual; Sheila-Na-Gig; The Ekphrastic Review* and *One Art*. She was awarded second place in the Belfast Maine Postmark Poetry Festival Contest 2023. She lives and plays in Maine.

Susan Beall Summers is a Texas Gulf Coast poet. She was a sheltered, naïve teen who came to appreciate Grateful Dead in college. Many friends were true Deadheads, and they filled her imagination with wild stories of following the band, the free carnival atmosphere, the interesting people, and fun experiences. Eventually, she became more Parrothead than Deadhead, and attending Bonaroo and Kerrville Folk Festival are the closest she has come to the Dead experience — so far.

J. Martin Strangeweather toured with the Grateful Dead in the late 80s and early 90s, attending approximately 300 concerts. He still enjoys the occasional Dead & Company show.

Chuck Taylor spent a lot of days hiking the Lone Star Trail in the San Houston National Forest, or canoeing in the far north end of Lake Conroe. Those were places of sacred solitude. He enjoyed people especially at Rainbow Gatherings and at Dead Concerts.

Tommy Twilite is a Massachusetts troubadour who combines music, poetry, exploration and adventure into his performances. He is the co-founder and director of the Florence Poets Society and the host of the Twilite Poetry Pub on WXOJ Valley Free Radio. His latest chapbook, "Kills No Bird" is a follow up to his 2021 collection, "Fifty Words for Rain". Tommy Twilite is well known as someone who can transport an audience to another realm with his words and music. He was recently honored by the National Baseball Poetry Festival for his poem, "The Tools of Ignorance". Tommy is the editor of the Silkworm annual review, and is a Lifetime Beat Poet Laureate. He believes poetry and song can renew the Earth, and the Dead will always be grateful.

Karen A VandenBos was born on a warm July morn in Kalamazoo, MI. She has a PhD in Holistic Health where a course in shamanism taught her to travel between two worlds, those of the living and those of the dead. It was in the 70's when she was turned onto the Grateful Dead and she continues to tend to them as she travels through time. Karen can be found unleashing her imagination in two online writing groups. A Best of the Net nominee, her writing has been published in *Lothlorien Poetry Journal, Blue Heron Review, The Rye Whiskey Review, One Art: a journal of poetry, Anti-Heroin Chic, The Ekphrastic Review, Southern Arizona Press, MacQueen's Quinterly, Moss Piglet, Panoply, Peninsula Poets* and others.

Lenore Weiss serves as the Associate Creative Nonfiction (CNF) Editor for the *Mud Season Review* and lives in Oakland, California with Zebra the Brave and Granola the Shy. Her environmental novel *Pulp into Paper* was published this year on Earth Day as was a new poetry collection, *Video Game Pointers* from WordTech Communications.

Lynn White is dead grateful to have lived in the time of the coolest music ever! She presently resides in north Wales and her work is influenced by issues of social justice and events, places and people she has known or imagined. She is especially interested in exploring the boundaries of dream, fantasy and reality. She has been nominated for a Pushcart Prize, Best of the Net and a Rhysling Award. https://lynnwhitepoetry.blogspot.com and https://www.facebook.com/Lynn-White-Poetry-1603675983213077/

Poet, writer, editor, publisher, professor, scholar, activist, U.S. National Lifetime Beat Poet Laureate **Ron Whitehead** is the author of 30 books and 40 albums. A UNESCO Europe Writer-in-Residence, his work has been translated into 20 languages. The City of Louisville presented him with a Lifetime Achievement Award for his work in The Arts. He has been nominated for the Pulitzer and the Nobel Prize in Literature. He has produced thousands of music and poetry events, festivals, and Insomniacathons across Europe and the USA. In May 2024 he produced his 3rd 24-hour non-stop music & poetry Insomniacathon in Estonia. In July 2024 he produced The Last Insomniacathon, a 57-hour non-stop music & poetry & arts happening, at the Chapel of St. Philip Neri in Louisville. At 73, he continues to perform and record with The Storm Generation Band and many others. His newest book, *TAPPING MY OWN PHONE*, was just released by the National & International Beat Poetry Foundation. *OUTLAW POET: The Legend of Ron Whitehead* (Storm Generation Films/Dark Star TV), a feature length documentary on Ron's life and work, is now available for streaming on Amazon Prime Films Documentaries.

D.A. "Roarshock" Wilson is a Northern California poet and storyteller. Publisher of San Francisco's ROARSHOCK PAGE a literary street flier, and author of FIRST HOURS OF A RAINY DAY AND OTHER POEMS. He has performed Spoken Word for many years in diverse venues, locally and internationally.

He joined the global online poetry revival beginning in March 2020 which has greatly expanded his audience and circle of fellow poets. Currently he is Co-host of the weekly social web reading Spoken World Online (the global local iteration of Spoken Word Paris). He can be found online at http://www.roarshock.net

"Catfish John" Wojtowicz grew up working on his family's azalea and rhododendron nursery and still lives in the backwoods of what Ginsberg dubbed "nowhere Zen New Jersey." Currently, he teaches social work at his local community college. The music of the Grateful Dead and the Deadhead community continues to help him find direction, acceptance, and his dancing shoes. He is the author of the chapbook, *Roadside Attractions: a Poetic Guide to American Oddities*. Find out more at: www.johntiojtowicz.com

Elizabeth S. Wolf has published 5 books of poetry. Her memoir chapbook *Did You Know?* was a *Rattle* prize winner. Selected works are included in the *Lunar Codex Nova Collection*, an archive that landed on the moon. She's happily retired in Massachusetts.

Uzomah Ugwu is a poet/writer, curator, editor, and multi-disciplined artist. Her poetry, writing, and art have been featured internationally in various publications, galleries, art spaces, and museums. She is a political, social, and cultural activist. Her core focus is on human rights, mental health, animal rights, and the rights of LGBTQIA persons. She is also the managing editor and founder of *Arte Realizzata*. She considers herself and her creative process to be that of a social disrupter.

EDITOR BIO

D.L. Lang is a former poet laureate of Vallejo, California. Lang has been listening to the Grateful Dead since she was a teenager in Oklahoma in the late '90s. She adores their folk inspired albums, *Workingman's Dead* and *American Beauty* the most. Her poetry has been used as liturgy, transformed into songs, and used to advocate for peace, justice, and a better world. Lang is an internationally published poet whose work appears in over 80 anthologies. As a winner of the 2023 Curbside Haiku Contest, her haiku was displayed across downtown Tulsa and is archived at the Woody Guthrie Center. She is a member of the Revolutionary Poets Brigade, a two time Woody Guthrie Poet, and a co-founder of the Vallejo Poetry Society. Lang was recognized by the California State Senate and California Arts Council for her service as poet laureate. She has performed hundreds of times at festivals, demonstrations and literary events. Find out more at poetryebook.com

ACKNOWLEDGMENTS

- "If," "Graceland," and "Gone" by B. Elizabeth Beck are reprinted from *Dancing on the Page* (Rabbit House Press, 2024)
- "There is a Doppelgänger Planet" by Trish Hopkinson was first published in *Lost at 27: Musicians, Artists, Mortals* (Cicada Song Press, 2024)
- "My Brother who I only See at Dead Shows" by PW Covington was first published in the UK by Coin- Operated Press, in their 'Subcultures' edition.
- "Ripple" by Pesach Rotem was first published in Nine Mile Art & Literary Magazine, Fall 2018, volume 6, issue 1.
- "Rolling Papers, Pipes, Bongs, Roach clips" by Ron Whitehead appeared in *Gregory Corso: Ten Times A Poet* (Roadside Press).
- "The Question That Killed Cassady" appears on Air Lift Underground's first album, *No Mind Left Unblown* (nomindleft.com). Reprinted with permission.

HOW TO MAKE BREAKFAST OR WHATEVER WHILE FOLLOWING A TOUR ALL SUMMER BY JULEIGH HOWARD-HOBSON

My old deadhead friend says iron's the best
but, whatever, you can use any sort
of pan or pot. Even a griddle. (Test,
first, he cautions, how much it holds, to work
out any bummers beforehand), Then, he
says, break five or six eggs and mix them all
up, add crumbs of cheese and little trippy
treats like mushrooms, or infinitesimal
bits of hash or other stuff. Pour this
into the iron pan, or pot, or what
ever you are using. Now, with a whisk,
or spoon, quickly stir and stir as your pot
of food cooks up into a far-out mess
of scrambled eggs. Share all that grooviness.

THE GRATEFUL DEAD IS FAMILY BY HANNAH LIEBREICH

Dedicated to my nephew JJ Garcia on his 2nd birthday

The Grateful Dead means playing my plastic guitar while dad plays
"Mr. Tambourine Man."
And it's mom making spaghetti and salad for dinner while she listens to
tunes.

The Grateful Dead means "Friend of the Devil" on the juke box and
dancing on tabletops.
And it's Bobby playing "Bird Song" in Charlotte for two sisters mourning
their mom.

The Grateful Dead means "I'm not really a dead head, but my dad is."
And it's driving twelve hours home to Ohio for Hyryder's second set at
Stanley's Pub.

The Grateful Dead means "Box of Rain" on repeat while my baby nephew
calms down.
And it's a soothing slow dance while he drifts back into sleep.

The Grateful Dead means Thursday's Dead on a Sunday at the
Grand Strand Brewery.
And it's feeling a little less alone in a city that feels so lonely.

But the Grateful Dead is never *really* feeling alone
because there's always a band in a bar somewhere, making sure the music
lives on.

THE DAY EVERYTHING CHANGED BY K.LIPSCHUTZ

I can close my eyes and see them clearly,
holding up a wall at Masonic & Haight,
or cross-legged on the grass
at the mouth of Golden Gate Park,
guys (mostly) who never recovered
from smoking a joint with Jerry Garcia,
who spent the inheritance of their days
wondering what current, what currency
their saliva had exchanged.

DREAMSHIP BY BENGT O BJÖRKLUND

A few years ago
I dreamt I was on a cruise ship
on my way to Finland.
On deck I saw Jerry Garcia
and Bob Weir looking at me.
Bob said: "Hi, Bengt!" smiling.
I said: "Hi, Bob!"
then I woke up.
I wasn't going with that ship.

GARCIA IS WAITING 'TIL TOMORROW COMES BY JUDE BRIGLEY

So, Nash gave you an alligator guitar
in return for the steel of "Teach your
Children." It made the track ascend,

spiraling in domestic bliss. And it
was easy to hear a plea to wait
for morning and to lose footsteps

in the dark and snow. You knew
them all – Joplin, Ginsberg, Swami,
Dylan. All along the watchtower,

you improvised the going, going,
gone. The Dead love syncopation.
You were the mixing eclectic –

loving Django and Duke, Benson
and Davis, switching scales,
capturing ragas, referencing

the mediaeval and folklore.
The Cherry is more than a pun-
it's a tribute. Its smooth

ice-cream evokes your melodic
moods, the fruit and chocolate
mixing genre, gratefully received.

RIPPLE ON THE ROAD BY CHANDER DHINGRA

In the echo of strings, where the mountains rise,
a highway hums beneath wild skies.
The Dead play on in a timeless sway,
their notes, like rivers, flow and stray.
A strum, a hum, and the world unwinds,
casting off weight, leaving worries behind.
In the rhythm of life, a story is told,
of love and loss, and dreams of gold.
Phil's bass line trembles through my soul,
while Jerry's riffs make me feel whole.
In a thousand faces, I see the same.
We're all searching, dancing in the flame.
Under the stars, where the wind does shift,
time slows down in the Dead's sweet drift.
A ripple spreads, unseen, unheard.
In every note, there's a whispered word.
In the music's embrace, I find my home
on roads unmarked where Deadheads roam.
For every song is a journey, no end, no start,
just the beat of the band in tune with my heart.

TO STRING A CROWN OF SWEET SCARLET BEGONIAS UPON ME BY APRIL RIDGE

I was freshly 14 the year that Jerry Garcia died.

Just back after my first summer as a reckless teenager
who had run away from home.
Sporting a duffle bag and a small brown suitcase
stuffed full of cutouts from *Rolling Stone* and *Spin Magazine*
whistlin' "On the Road Again."

Jerry Garcia, The Beatles, Kurt Cobain, Tom Petty Beck,
Sonic Youth, Hole, The Cranberries:
they all traveled with me to unknown destinations that summer
as I ran away from who I didn't want to become.

Some forlorn prisoner in the school system,
lotted out to be just another bored, unchallenged kid bouncing off the walls
that couldn't pay any attention to some bullshit algebra
the higher ups deemed necessary to form a well-rounded education.
I played *Europe '72* over and over in foam-coated headphones
eaten away by love, peace and years and years of hair grease.

Jerry died the week we got caught in Elkhart, Indiana, but we hadn't heard.

The cops bashed the wooden door in on someone's uncle's house that
we were crashing at for the night.
The deadbolt useless, dangling in the midnight hour.

Two runaway girls with two way-too-old men accompanying them.
I was asleep in a recliner when they started to knock,
my girlfriend, 13, with a new rattail haircut and dye job,
and her boyfriend passed out on the matted carpet floor.
The uncle probably leering, reeling drunk,
from some unknown dark corner.
There was no way to escape, so we just stood by the door,
waiting to be beckoned home.

They wouldn't let me take my bags.
The suitcase and all its rock n rollers abandoned
like some easy wind passed on down the road.
We were taken to a jail just inside the downtown square,
as they didn't have a juvenile center.

They shackled us together, fed us cold beans and
2 day old bread laid out for youngsters who needed a lesson.
They told my family I'd been assaulted by the men (I hadn't).
Released into an aunt's neurotic custody.
One more week of freedom!!
Allowed to chain smoke and laze around in her place
while awaiting my true sentence.

I returned home, defiant and triumphant,
knowing *EVERYTHING*, as 14 year olds always do.
Mom tried to punish, but she was too much of a friend that year.

Should have locked me away for a while.
Would have done me good.

That first night back, I tried acid for the first time.
We lived across the street from the Wabash River, and
a city park flooded with the early bird leaves of a coming fall.
We traipsed about the familiar streets, eyeing everything,
doing nothing, but relishing in its significance.

That next morning, I found out that Jerry Garcia had died.

Contemplating the sadness I had
that I didn't fully understand at such a young age,
that I'd missed out on the big dream.
There **was** no true shakedown street waiting
just downstream for me.
The dream was gone. The band retired backstage permanently.

I was a strung out mess,
young and in a rut of some feverish dream.
I felt old in my youth, felt the sting of time passing.
How fragile, how precarious life can be
for those living, trying to balance themselves
on the high ledge of fame, self-medication, and the weight of it *allllll*
goin down the road, feelin' bad.

I drifted off to sleep thinking
one day, I'll climb Franklin's tower
in that brokedown palace,
Black Peter waiting there
to string a crown of sweet scarlet begonias upon me.

JUST ONE MORE SATURDAY NIGHT BY KAREN A VANDENBOS

The electric kool-aid acid test was the prelude to one more Saturday night, the night when Sugar Magnolia would take a spin on the wavy dance floor with Tennessee Jed and the notes from the "Cumberland Blues" would float out the open windows.

In a dark corner of the bar Mr. Charlie sat with Jack Straw and cut a deal with Casey Jones over a brown eyed woman who sipped Ripple wine from a vase of China cat sunflower. Quietly she looked the men in the eye and whispered, "You win again."

In the parking lot Ramble on Rose crept up to a school bus called Furthur, and said, "I know you, rider," before she was swept away on a ship of fools. It was such a long strange trip she thought it was her own fare thee well tour.

At the hour of closing time when the full moon rose like an epilogue against a starless canvas, a wharf rat consorted with Scarlet Begonias and turned her into a friend of the devil while he danced with merry pranksters and dared to call Sugaree his darlin' after swallowing the magic cast by the warlocks.

When a dark star erupted in the night sky Mountain Girl softly sang he's gone and heard Bear acknowledge that it hurts me, too. As the sun burst from the fire on the mountain they walked into the morning dew and kept truckin' towards another brokedown palace where they would forever continue to drink the kool-aid and tend to their dead.

JUST DON'T CALL IT FRISCO BY JAY PASSER

Jello and Jerry
belly up to the bar—
both agree that
antidisestablishmentarianism
is a very big word.

I caught the Dead at the Greek in Bezerkley
then the DKs at the Mabuhay on Broadway
on a single fateful weekend in 1984;
the year Orwell pegged for ultimate totalitarian rule
by cunningly switching the digits of the number 48.

Hey man, you can take that bit of minutiae and... um... uh... whoa, lost
my train of thought...
That's cool, Cap'n Trips...
Y'know, I was a punk before you were a punk, son...
Wasn't it Fee Waybill who said that?
Don't get smart with me, kid...

My patchouli-fragranced girlfriend with Birkenstocks and wisps of
blonde peeking out her shortsleeved paisley t-shirt admonished me:
Eww! Why so stinky! Get out of my bed! You need to hose off...

The Eddies slapped their tats, swallowed their smokes, punched their fists,
stomped their Docs, the anarchist A scrawled in crimson on their foreheads:
Ya dirty hippie wanker! Where ya been? Woodstock? Why don't ya fuck
off and die!

I talk to myself at times:
Hey! It's not about the look, or any particular style of music- punk is an
ethos... It's not who I am underneath, but what I *do*, that defines me...

Dude! Didn't Batman say that?
All I'd get from smashing that bastard in the mirror
is 7 years of bad luck,
so naturally,
I shave my glass jaw in the shower.

THE QUESTION THAT KILLED CASSADY BY AIRLIFT UNDERGROUND

Codified bridge from beat to hippie,
A rudderless vessel of psychedelic discovery,
Unclean machine of perpetual perversity,
Transiting between altered states and cities
Fueled by sweaty adrenaline
And wanderlusty audacity.
Skin blistering with palpitating authenticity,
Oozing sexuality and howling holy obscenities
Under an umbrella of numinous luminosity.

Scribbling notes along the envelope's edge,
Twinkling between the rock of a twisted fix
And the hard place of standing still
A high wire daredevil driving a Tight rope,
Reading *I Ching* and levitating twenty steel tons
Another wild mad dash Furthur up Highway 1,
Burning benzedrine, LSD, and destiny,
Bearing Dean Moriarty's *On The Road* legacy.

Scraping handlebar guardrails,
Rambling through every rubber-burning turn,
Bopping to the beat of a different apocalypse, Seven-pointed star with lightning lips,
Careening through rag-tag jazz manuscripts,
Reeling off an unseen screen,
Switching scenes between half a dozen twisted flicks,
Behind the wheel of the big reveal,
At the helm of the bus that launched ten thousand trips.

Well, Cowboy Neal was a curious cat,
A cameo character with a craning neck,
Jaunting through panoramic habitats,
Hand dealt from the underside of the deck,
Rolling out the film in reverse.
Drunkard orphan hitching the skids
Toward the outskirts of the Universe.
They say feline lives number nine.
Cassady ran through them three at a time.
The first third flying by at high velocity.
The second third the reborn bon vivant of literary immortality.
The third third cut short by the fall of a curtain call.
Yeah, the third third of that cat's tale. Well, that didn't happen at all.
Feline lives, they come in nines,
But how many railroad ties
Is it to the end of the line?

It's the question that killed Neal Cassady.
What glitters in the corner of all I see?
Past yesterday's unfettered artistry
Behind the rat-a-tat patter of the acid test barker
And wry grin of the irrepressible skylarker,
Rapping off a scatter-shot branched narrative,
Dripping with hedonism and vainglory.
It's the metastasized story of a reformatory refugee,
Chasing an insatiable curiosity.
Well, they say curiosity is what killed the cat,
But, baby, satisfaction is what brought him back.

Get a load of this sensational sensation.
Groove on that wonderstruck unstuck vibration.
Hang up those hang-ups and grab the phone.
There's a call for you from the great unknown.
Notions in motion on waves of "maybe" and "let's see."
The core of Aporia, the glory of all that happens to be.
Boundless novelty over yonder horizon.
A maze of labyrinthine amazement.
Accumulated cumulus clouds cushioning the searing Sun
Under myriad piercing gazes conjuring allegorical fantasies,
Crystallized visions dug up to resurrect
Sights and sounds and synesthetic scents.
No mind left unblown.
No line left unbent.

Dig it, digits, with opposable thumbs,
Jutting out to beckon whatever may come
Wrapped up in tarpaulin folds of undertow,
And tidal flows of who knows where it's gonna go.
Packed in the back of Serendipity's pick-up jalopy,
Following the fortunes of random roadside processions,
Cosmos shattered through dew-drop prismed progressions,
Unlocking spectral rainbows trapped inside indifferent infinity,
Sun-spun cycles of last chances and first impressions,
Melodies plucked from moaning droned tonalities,
Unfolding untold golden eternities.

Electrified steel-wrought mechanical dreams
Stoked on the steam from locomotive combustion,
Meeting each moment beneath a scalding stream
Of quantum kinetic connotative implications.
Multi-faceted visceral crystal-shard rings
Trembling in orbit around Cassady's question,
Ripping the fabric of the grace-slime continuum.
Sinless, schizo-maniacal saint of the strange
Marking space, time, and novel conundrums
Across whatever remains of the vanishing free range.
Psychedelic skipper sailing through the Big Dipper
Seekin' All Seekin' All....

Was it ultimately the quest
Or just the ultimate question
That finally did unkneeling Cassady in?

Oh, the question that killed Neal Cassady.
How far to that city he would never see?
They say feline lives number nine.
Cassady ran through them three at a time
Chasing that terminal curiosity.
Notions in motion on waves of "maybe" and "let's see."
The core of Aporia, the glory of all that will ever be.
Feline lives, they come in nines,
But how many railroad ties is it, is it, is it,
How many railroad ties is it to the end of the line?
Well, they say curiosity is what killed the cat,
But, baby, satisfaction is what brought him back,
And so the question came and went.
No mind left unblown.
No line left unbent.

— Lyrics by Amana Mission and Indi Riverflow

IF BY B. ELIZABETH BECK

we would have been best friends, probably why I bark laugher of recognition,
hearing these lyrics. At eighteen, I knew there was absolutely nothing happening at all,
       yet everything
was. Jerry Garcia shines his love light & I follow—the world melts away as I enter
a universe I've yet to abandon, grateful every note cradles my broken soul, relieved to
       feel
at home when I have no other, open to receiving love when strangers stop strangers
& roses are free, all stemming from a simple song I discover in a college art studio.
In those days, I said everything I wanted to say with a brush on canvas, seeking truth
       in blades
of grass, following Holden Caulfield, studying psychedelic clouds, finding Lucy's
diamonds. My first dance steps in front of television, a toddler walking as if on a bubble
as Neil Armstrong lands on the moon, after Neal Cassady drives the bus I get on,
       escaping
parents who should have been the death of us all. I'm still wondering how I'm alive.

Reprinted from Dancing on the Page (Rabbit House Press, 2024)

THERE IS A DOPPELGÄNGER PLANET BY TRISH HOPKINSON
where rock stars don't die
when they're twenty-seven

& addiction rolls off new skin
like oil in a hot skillet   unable to cling

unable to soak in   twenty-somethings
who take in too much   take in sky instead

—the pulse of dove wings
   in the ripples of the river's edge

take in the rush of breath
through nostrils primed   the incense

of electric rain & early dew   palm at the small
of the back   guiding but   staying behind

never too many   too young—
wrapped in drudgery so taut   no glimmer

can squeak through   on this doppelgänger
planet   we glance about unsure

of whom we will become   hand our tickets
   to be torn & kneel on the lawn

as Jimi, Janis, Jim & PigPen belt
on an open air stage   even as their necks

fold and crease, fingers curl, lips thin—
     hair catching white in starlight

First published in Lost at 27: Musicians, Artists, Mortals (Cicada Song Press, 2024)

A LONG STRANGE TRIP BY BARRIE PATTON

One day, during the cold rain and snowy season, me and my uncle were listening to the bird song as we were walking beside the black muddy river. We were just throwing stones to watch the water ripple when we happened upon two friends, Bertha and Cassidy.

They were very distressed, saying, "We feel like we've been walking down desolation row for so long searching but, he's gone, he's just gone!"

We asked "What's the deal, ladies? Are you ok?"

They said they have been going down the road, but feeling bad, because they can't find the candyman, anywhere!

We told them we will provide help on the way.

They told us the last time they had spoken to Mr. Charlie, he said that he saw him near the broke down palace, dancing in the streets.

We knew what we had to do! We had to go see the big boss man—the one they call the eyes of the world! So we beat it on down the line all the way to El Paso, but we had to hurry 'cause it looks like rain! So we headed out to the new speedway and boogied! We met a few very interesting people along the way who all had a story as to where the candyman could be.

We ran into Jed from Tennessee who told us we should go see the lady with a fan over at Terrapin Station. She may know where he is.

Then we ran into the other one, Peggy O. She sat holding a China cat in one hand and China doll in in the other hand while she told us all about her foolish heart. She said she had fallen for a guy who once said to her, "I will take you home," but he turned out to be a loser.

We reminded her that we are all going to hell in a bucket, and she was better off without him! We told her, "There comes a time when we don't worry about the days in between, and one day we will all be standing on the moon, where no one would ever feel like a stranger again!"

As we hugged her she had said we made her remember what good lovin' was all about. She told us to walk quietly, like cats down under the stars, 'til we hear the little red rooster, then we will know we are close!

Next we met up with Stella Blue. She is the one they call the estimated prophet. She was a brown eyed woman—oh, just so beautiful with scarlet begonias in her hair. She spoke in almost a riddle when she said to us, "If I had the world to give, I'd give it from the heart of me, I'll tell you where the boss man is, but you must use caution. As you head toward the sunrise, watch out for the alligator, then head down the road to unlimited devotion!"

Then we all looked up as she exclaimed, "Look! Here comes sunshine now! You better get going."

We felt like we were sitting on top of the world! But it was high time we shook our bones and went.

As we walked along the golden road, we saw a smokestack that had lightning all around it. It was right near Franklin's Tower. (That thing was built to last!) But could that be where he was?! We needed a miracle, and this was turning out to be the greatest story ever told!

We walked around and around, near a big river. After a while it felt like we had a hundred thousand tons of steal on our backs! And then, a big gust of black throated wind blew, kicking up dust and dirt. When the dust cleared, we saw that we had made it! We found the big boss man!! He was kinda like a wharf rat, who had been born cross eyed, with these crazy fingers and just a touch of grey in his hair, and he seemed to know where the candyman was.

He told us he had seen a fire on the mountain, and that is where we will find him. He then told us to follow the dark star down the dark hollows, 'til we saw the mountains of the moon. We did as he instructed, and began to climb up. (At one point we ran into a dire wolf! Man, that was scary!)

Then, finally, we met the candyman! He was a wise old fella who told us how he had been all around this world.

He told us how he spent his 21st birthday in prison for what he says was "just a spoonful of cocaine." He admitted how hard his mama tried with him and then said, "I feel that she is so far from me now."

He told us how she had this long blond hair that always smelled like flowers. As was he remembering the very essence of her, he just sighed and said, "It must have been the roses."

There was this one point, where we heard a distant drumming—the most amazing sounds we have ever heard. It was as if the devils had rhythm! We are pretty sure this was Uncle John's band. Candyman man got all spacey during that 45 minute time period.

When he awoke from this almost trance-like state he was in, he was in another zone. He told us to hold onto that unbroken chain, because that slipknot may not hold till the morning comes. He told us how to handle our gardens. He said to just let it grow, make sure they face the sunrise, and don't be fooled by fake herbs that look like rosemary, but are not. He told us to turn on our love light, that we just need a little light, not money money, and then we will win again! He said, "I know you rider, remember death don't have no mercy, so wait till the morning comes when the morning dew, is on the ground and you will finally see the promised land!"

We spent a long time with him, he had the best advice and even better stash! But alas, it was time to head into that easy wind, and bid him goodnight.

We spun our wheels and went trucking all the way back to the pride of Cucamonga where we finally felt some peace and rested our weary bones thankful we were all just a passenger on this long strange trip!

GRACELAND BY B. ELIZABETH BECK

we sing with Paul Simon, driving
a Chevy to the Pyramid, stopping

to hover at wax Elvis behind gate
who reappears at show, stripping clothes

as police on horses divide deadheads
from Beale Street drunken revelry

not as weird as Detroit when the dome
lifts, stars, and planets descend

during drums and space I do not
realize is psychedelic illusion

familiar dream state in Indiana
cornfields, seeking Sleepy Bear

or gold wing bikers in Louisville
without the sting of Hell's Angels

we were too young for Woodstock
but old enough to get on the bus

Reprinted from *Dancing on the Page* (Rabbit House Press, 2024)

ROLLING PAPERS, PIPES, BONGS, ROACH CLIPS BY RON WHITEHEAD

Part 1: How IT Started

We'd finished our 2nd 5th of Southern Comfort and the mescaline was kicking in. Jimi Hendrix crosses borders, threatening to ascend towards heaven. With lightning and thunder he plays Bob Dylan's "All Along The Watchtower." Stereo loud as it will go.

Here in the only underground bookstore in Kentucky: For Madmen Only. Shelves and bins stocked with books and records from City Lights and bookpeople in San Francisco and from Atlantis and Alligator in New Orleans. Teas and herbs and candles from mountain communes. Turquoise blue Spiritual Sky incense. And next door in The Store, our Head Shop, paraphernalia: rolling papers, pipes, bongs, roach clips, water beds, posters, GROW YOUR OWN: How To Pamphlets, plus blankets and clothes from India, Native American jewelry, and more. We're serving the new consciousness. Inspired by the one and only King of The Dharma Bums: Jack Kerouac, and

Lawrence Ferlinghetti, Gary Snyder, Richard Brautigan, Ken Kesey, Neal Cassady, Allen Ginsberg, Gregory Corso, William Carlos Williams, William Blake, Hermann Hesse, Knut Hamsun, Dostoevsky, Nietzsche, Bukowski, Thomas Merton, The Dalai Lama, Gandhi, Burroughs, LeRoi Jones, Diane di Prima, Hunter S. Thompson, Ralph Steadman, with Robert Johnson, Hound Dog Taylor, Howlin' Wolf, Jimi Hendrix, The Grateful Dead, Left Zeppelin, and always Bob Dylan, Bob Dylan, Bob Dylan on the stereo.

But we're Down and Out in Kentucky, failing like no others dare fail, and we're always on the outside, outsiders, outlaws, being told, "You don't fit! You ain't shit! What the fuck you doing here?!"

And so *On The Road* is where we live, traveling, traveling, traveling. A band of gypsies in search of IT, headed out of Kentucky, across the USA: coast to coast, ghost to ghost, down to Mexico, determined to keep on keeping on, trucking till the wheels fall off and burn. Just passing through. Searching, searching.

Yes, after all these years still searching for IT, and yet somewhere, somehow, one day, one moment, at the heights of Machu Picchu, we went further in, traveled deeper on the inner road. We entered The 3rd Kingdom, The 4th Dimension where lies the synthesis of apparently irreconcilable differences. And in the heart of The Big Bang Epiphany we discovered that the power and the glory of IT is bound in the grace of forgiveness, of Beating Karma through love and compassion by persevering through desperate circumstances.

So now we GO GO GO. We Never Give Up, We realize Now that The Road, Jack Kerouac's Road, our Road always leads On so ever Furthur we GO GO GO.
And I was gone, baby, gone.

Part 2: On The Road with Gregory

Years later, still on the road:

In 1993 I was invited to read with Gregory Corso at the Lowell Celebrates Kerouac Festival, so I rented a big passenger van and loaded up my kids, who went on so many adventures with me, and friends and posters and chapbooks and books and albums then drove fast all through the dark night to New York City arriving at dawn to Allen Ginsberg's apartment. We visited with Allen and Diane di Prima, who was staying with Allen for a few days, then I called Gregory to let him know I was on my way to pick him up.

Gregory said, "No, I can't go. Not without a hundred dollars so I can buy some necessary supplies."

I said, "Gregory, I don't really have the money, but okay, I'll find it. We've got to get on the road."

He said, "Come on. Let's go. It'll only take me a few minutes to gather what I need for the trip." I knew what that meant. On the four hour drive from New York City to Lowell, Massachusetts. Corso asks questions and tells stories. When we walk into the Lowell hotel lobby Michael McClure and Ray Manzarek yell and wave for us to come over. Corso, McClure, and Manzarek all knew each other so I introduced myself and let them know that Gregory and I were reading that evening. Manzarek asked me where I was from.

I said, "Kentucky." McClure said, "Diane di Prima speaks highly of you." Then I quickly shared with them a little of my own history, and I preached some of the Global Literary Renaissance Gospel. We all talked for a few minutes then Gregory said, "I've got to get up to my room and take care of some business."

When I turned to leave with Gregory, Michael said, "Ron, wait. Let's talk some more." When Corso was out of ear shot McClure said, "I'll give you a hundred dollar bill if you keep Gregory away from our performance."

I looked at him then laughed and said, "I don't have any control over Gregory. Nobody does, but I'll do what I can." Gregory had a reputation of hatefully heckling other performers. Ray Manzarek was a nice guy, a gentleman. Later in the afternoon I gathered everyone for a visit to Kerouac's grave, before our reading. On our way we drove by the club where we'd be performing.

Corso yelled, "Stop! I've got to have a drink."

I said, "Gregory, we don't have time."

Gregory said, "I'll hurry. I'll be right back."

I said, "Okay. I'll go with you."

The place was packed. As we entered everyone turned and, seeing Gregory Corso, grew quiet. A path opened for us to get to the bar. As the bartender came over to take our order, a guy at the bar said, "Hey, you're Gregory Corso. You heckled Diane di Prima at her reading. I'm gonna whip your ass." Corso turned white as a ghost then he started growling. Corso didn't take shit off anybody.

I stepped between Gregory and the drunk at the bar. I looked at the bartender and said, "Hey, this idiot wants to fight Gregory Corso. He needs to get the hell outta here!"

In a heartbeat two bartenders grabbed the guy and tossed him out. Folks said he should've been thrown out earlier. We ordered our drinks. John Sampas and his brother yelled at us to come over to their table.

They offered to buy us drinks and dinner. I thanked them but told them I had a van load of folks and we're headed to visit Kerouac's grave before the show. Corso accepted their offer and stayed.

At Jack Kerouac's grave I called on his spirit inviting him to join our performance offering him Southern hospitality in Lowell, Massachusetts. As I summoned Jack's spirit I felt the wind pick up and orange and yellow October leaves began to dance and swirl about and with us there at Saint Kerouac's grave.

Back at the club I felt his spirit grow stronger as I presented my reading to a packed house. When I was done I introduced Gregory Corso. No sound. When I looked over to his table Corso let out a pleading moan saying, "I can't. I'm too fucked up. I've got to go back to the hotel." I asked two friends to help Gregory back to the hotel. The room was silent as Corso stumbled away.

An earlier version of this also appeared in Gregory Corso: Ten Times A Poet (Roadside Press).

GRATEFUL DEAD, LSD & POETRY BROKE MY CHAIN BY CLAIRE CONROY

Lyric poem from "Unbroken Chain"

I was blue. Light rain fell in my teenage years.
Death had left an empty window pane.
Searching for the sound I needed to hear,
but the baying of his hounds left me insane.

In a willow sky I sought visions to get lost.
They say, "LOVE!" so I adopted the lullaby...
Roll me down the line, constellations star-crossed
out on a cold night where my thoughts could fly.

Through sounds and more, as I soar with pleasure,
I found my forgiveness is the key to atone.
Seeds bloomed into flowers in a night like forever.
Through the music my doubts sank like a stone.

Lilac rain on my tongue unleashed a wreath of curls
of the winds howling around my head.
These melodies broke my chain of sorrow and pearls.
The western wind had brought in my Grateful Dead.

WHEN THEY WERE YOUNG BY CHRIS DEAN

20 years too late
to be 19 at Woodstock,
too young to understand
the heartbeat of silver and gray,
a mother too soon
to follow the revival,
the music, more than blood,
sugar in my veins.

uncle john and friendly devils,
my pied pipers calling the tune,
calling the dance
with the simple word:
freedom,
from scratchy records,
ripples of truth.

we danced in the living room
ring-around-the-rosey,
tie-dyes and beads,
bare feet thumping wood floors
hippie children taught
a longing for going,
knowing all the words
before they're knew how to talk.

they went their way,
too late to go mine,
the time of growing up came,
and something died as it passed,
memories and music,
sweet smell of blossoms
remind me
of freedom's dreams
when they were young.

GRATEFULLY BY MARK LIPMAN

Gratefully,
after all this time
everything seems alright.
there's no need to worry.
what will be will be,
and as long as I live,
I just keep moving
in the direction
I need to go.

Every problem
has multiple solutions.
it all just depends
on how you face it
head on or running scared.

If they haven't found
a way to kill you yet,
you might as well take
a chance on living.

At least get out the door,
light up and look all around.

There's a whole world out there
waiting to be discovered,
ready to welcome you.

Whether on shakedown street
in the dark of midnight
or dancing with bears
to the fire on the mountain,
it's all a magic trip
as we're driving that train
comin' round the bend of life
with a touch of grey, as we still do

not fade away going down the road
like C.C. Rider on an acid trip,
making friends with the devil
and other cool cats along the way.

The point is the journey,
the experiences and friends
we make along the way to that
next great truck stop in the sky
as we just keep truckin' on
through that ripple of existence.

DEADHEADS FROM JERSEY BY "CATFISH JOHN" WOJTOWICZ

My road-dawg and I rode a gondola over the redwoods
at a tourist trap somewhere north
of the Avenue of the Giants
before my truck blew a belt on Highway 101.

We went from gliding like California condors
over evergreen behemoths
to camping under them in a nylon tent
like fungus sprouting from canopy soil.

Some friends of friends who struck gold in the green-rush
came from Oroville to Pistol River to rescue us
when we couldn't stomach the food
left floating in our cream cheese-contaminated cooler water.

Between us, my drug-rug-clad-compadre and I,
didn't have a stainless shirt,
but in the flash of our hosts' platinum
card: vagrants to Gold Country Casino VIPs.

An elevator took us to the top floor where we
were greeted by a personal waitstaff
and a panoramic view to watch the westward
sunset as a pianist played Tchaikovsky to our platters:

shrimp scampi, calamari, cream of crab,
porterhouse pork chops with rosemary
paired with an off-dry Roussanne
and palette cleansers: food-between-the-food.

We were still savoring coffee crème brûlée crumbs
from our unruly mustaches
when cherry-tops reflected
in the rearview of the fresh-from-the-repair-shop pickup.

"You going to need backup?" the officer's two-way

paged as he peered into the window;
"Nah, just a couple good-for-nothing,
Deadheads from Jersey," he responded over the radio.

BLUES FOR A LONG STRANGE TRIP BY CHANDER DHINGRA

The moon was high. The night was warm.
We danced through stardust, felt the storm.
Jerry's voice like velvet wine
Sang us through the endless time.
Phil laid the beat like a thunder's roll,
Each note a thunder, shaking soul.
With each refrain, the years unwind,
A timeless groove, a peace of mind.
From Fillmore nights to cosmic haze,
The Dead carried us through their maze.
In every chord, a spark, a dream—
Life's sweetest echoes on the stream.
The road goes on, but the music stays
A song that we'll hum for endless days.
In every beat the past still lives.
The gift that only music gives.

"Blues for a Long Strange Trip" was inspired by the Grateful Dead's iconic song "Scarlet Begonias" and a chance encounter with fellow Deadheads at a concert.

DREAMING WITH SAN FRANCISCO BY SUSAN BEALL SUMMERS

Many have loved you long and true
penned letters, books of poems.

I'm jealous of these documented love affairs,
the intimacy shared with many.

They praise your vigor, beauty, youth,
serene, lovely, bawdy and uncouth.
I, too, profess my affection.

You, rugged and gentle,
dangerous water, golden bridge,
faulty earth, expansive parks,

smiles, smells,
indulgences in art, music,
legendary work ethic.

Small enough to cuddle
in dark corners of intimate cafes,
opening worlds of imagination.

Because I dreamed with you,
I opened to love more generously
all people, cultures and ways of life.

More than anywhere else,
you taught me borders
of land, sea, country,
or mind
are arbitrary, shifting
finally dissipating like fog—
only love remains.

SAUSALITO GETAWAY BY OZ HARDWICK

We glide across the Bay, sunshine
on the dashboard and white clouds
waving goodbye and good luck,
smiling in the rear view mirror.

There's a sweet song on the radio,
of restless joy and all those old friends
waiting in the light with wine and dancing.
Turn it up and wind down the windows!

Smiling skeletons line the road,
thumbs outstretched and beat guitar cases
slung across their frugging shoulders,
each clutching a sign that reads Furthur.

Climb aboard, there's room for all!

And the way winds on, that same song playing,
and our wheels give way to golden wings,
and we soar like laughing angels
into a sky of tie-dyed blues.

TRAVELING TO THE DOCK OF THE BAY BY SUSAN BEALL SUMMERS

At the laundromat with a friend,
during the wash cycle
we were drinking at the bar next door.

After the third round of drinks,
tipsy, I transferred wet clothes to the dryer
pushed in the quarters.
Turning around, I was surprised to find a Krishna in a saffron robe
selling holographic pictures.

I bought painted boats at a marina
a place I'd never seen—perhaps
a conjured premonition

Back in the dark bar, singing,
"On the Dock of the Bay"

When the early-afternoon drunk
shouted, *and I never got there*—
I made a pact with myself:

I *will* get there.

Years later in San Francisco,
I found the colorful boats in the bay,
and noted how far I'd roamed.

HAIGHT-ASHBURY REVERIE BY CHANDER DHINGRA

There,
beneath the washed-out hues of San Francisco skies,
where the streets hum like ancient vinyl,
we walked,
we swayed.
The scent of patchouli mingled with the sound
of Jerry's guitar,
lacing the air with stories,
soaked in the acid rain of yesterday's dreams.
We were the seekers,
the wanderers,
lost in the shifting tides of time.
The Dead,
our compass—
their rhythms our north star.
Between laughter and light,
we found home in their echoes,
where the world turned slower,
and every note melted into the pavement.
Here,
in the reverie of Haight-Ashbury,
we became one with the music,
fading into the chords of eternity.

AT THE TRUCK STOP, 1974 BY WILLIAM BUTLER

flat lands are best for truckin' I guarantee
where the road endlessly hums anthems
spaced pavement cracks percuss
and
the right rear Tire maypops' promise
reveals itself
limpin' into a truck stop east of Enid
trippin' from Amarillo
smellin' burning rubber
while
18-wheelers fly high on the overpass
trailin' streamers of crepe paper
and the Dead on the 8 track is salvation
guy in a flannel shirt listens through the open door
"New Speedway Boogie" jumps on him
slams him into boogie'n
and
he grooves changing the tire
for a Mickey Mouse blotter
"Cumberland Blues" and he's cryin'
we watch his tears become the river
that he dreams of right there
while
squatting over the jack
and
"Casey Jones" drives us to Tulsa
2 hours later
just in time to load in for our show
our heads fried
satisfied
our Dead are just ahead!

MY LIFE IN LYRICS BY ELIZABETH S. WOLF

My boyfriend jumped like a Willys in 4-wheel drive.
He was my summer love, spring, fall, and winter.
Our doors of perception were blown open wide.
I thought he knew the way—that he would take me home.

I married a man once, a friend of the devil
with a dimpled grin, eyes that changed from
green to gray, but he didn't believe
in that box of rain, wind, and water.
And he was not kind.
The sunny side of the street got dark.
No one wants to be treated that way.

I have a daughter and I tell her
dance a few steps every single morning.
Dance, before you leave the house;
It changes the way you are in the world.
Dance, even staying snug at home;
It changes the way you live in your head.
You are the miracle, every day.
You are a miracle every day.

YOU'RE CASEY JONES TONIGHT BY SUSAN BEALL SUMMERS

American hero
folk song

casual reference
for which operator
would drive the coal cars
to fuel the power plant

"You're Casey Jones tonight"
was the assignment that
made him hum and smile
remembering youth, good times.

SUGAR TAKES THE WHEEL BY SUSAN BEALL SUMMERS

I had never pulled a trailer
but he was too drunk,
so I drove Highway 25, dark and hilly
pulling 3 tons of steel.
in a truck I had rarely driven.

Late night traffic
backed up behind us,
with few opportunities to pass.
I gripped the wheel in terror
on the edge of my seat
to reach the pedals

in cool fall air,
beads of sweat on my forehead
heart pounding for the 30-mile ride
home from the dirt track races.
The load pushed me down the hills
exceeding the speed limits and
new levels of distress

"Don't touch the brakes! You'll jackknife,"
he said, and we slowly chugged up the next hill
to honks, flashing headlights, and cussing.
He told me to ignore the others
"You're doing a great job, Sugar."

We made it home alive.

Sunday was spent accessing the damage
to the race car. In the shade of the old magnolia,
he and his brother talked Tires
and stabilizers, how to get more power
in the straightaway.

DELIBERATELY LOST BY SUSAN BEALL SUMMERS

Let the pavement roll under the tires
wander the fence line, travel the river bed,
take the ferry ride to the other side

With exhilaration, find yourself lost,
nowhere to go,
no deadlines, no demands

Lost in time, in space, breathe—
in dreams, in beauty,
pleasure, clarity.

Lost and far away
where the language is foreign,
strange, melodic.

Ignore the map, signposts, GPS,
lose touch with world pressure
too many demands:

Be like this, think like me,
be somewhere unpleasant on time
for someone's else's convenience....

Pause.
feel the wind let go and

fly.

WHY I MISSED THE GRATEFUL DEAD CONCERT AT THE OAKLAND COLISEUM BY LENORE WEISS

Any number of reasons including how I'd arrived at the Lake Merritt BART station staring at crazy kids dressed in Mardi Gras feathers, beads, and tie-dyed everything, drifting happily in clouds of sweet- smelling smoke; I didn't have Tickets, certainly not the right clothes, too late as I stood in the parking lot

disparaging Dionysian maenads wearing nose rings and lugging backpacks across the street to the Beaux Arts Auditorium, dead-heads shedding flowers and getting high in the stands, smoking & dancing, I didn't know how to be that carefree—remembered

digging ditches in the baked limestone of Los Naranjos, and collecting signatures at Union Square, swimming in the White Mountains of New Hampshire with men and women who told stories about the Abraham Lincoln Brigade,

but as I stood there with my car keys, wondered how I'd found myself working at the Bank of America writing documentation for ATMS, those new Automatic Teller Machines?

COLISEUM LOT, 12/18/93 BY PAUL CORMAN-ROBERTS

I.

The palm size ceramic planter
an exact replica of Jerry's unshaven face
from the second solo record
"Compliments"

apart from the tiny grow-holes
perforating his cheeks and chin
where the tiny shoots
would fill in the famous profile

It's a Garchia Pet. Geddit?

We trade a phat nug and a Sierra for it.
It will be stolen from our group house
within six months.

II.

Half an hour
from the time we get in line
to the time we reach the doors

We hand the Tickets over.
The Bill Graham staffer eyeballs them
licks a finger on her glove
runs it across the Ticket faces
and the ink smears
across the cheap paper.

These are counterfeit, you must leave this line

Our friends already inside the Coliseum
looking back at us
until three big yellow jackets in the door

get between us and them.

...but.... but...

YOU HAVE TO LEAVE THIS LINE NOW!

In retrospect
the guy who sold us the
tickets did seem nervous and twitchy
And ran away from us
when we asked if he had more tickets.

Now, we walk past everyone
who had been in line behind us
for the last thirty minutes.

The walk of shame isn't always about a one-night stand
but it's always about someone who got fucked.

III.

The best way to a new ticket plan
my Dead miracle brother tells me
 is to split a big balloon of NO2
while listening to "Eyes of the World."

In the chill particulate orange
light of a December sunset
everything I can see/hear/smell/taste
becomes an infinite echo of itself.

All these children in ponchos,
transported here not in VW busses
but in their parents BMW's and Mercedes

haggling with the vendors
with currency other than cash
like a two-thousand-year-old Judean role play

or a premonition of a hundred years from now.

The nitrous wears off but the energy has not.

IV.

In the heart of this breathing
squirming organism
we call the lot

everything gives off heat
even in the Winter.

A voice:
Miracle Brother's ears
pick it up like radar.

$50 dollars each
A young hippie hesitates.

"Two for tonight?
I've got your $100 right here!"
Dead Miracle brother
lands the ship of fools.

A young hippie
with his girlfriend
walks away, head down.

A shift has occurred.
One head gathers what another leaves
at the playing table.

And somehow
my first show ever
becomes thirty-five.

HIGHGATE VERMONT SUMMER TOUR JULY 1994 BY ELIZABETH S. WOLF

My last Dead show I went as a guide. I was a grad student and my advisor had a 14 year old daughter. The daughter wore cowboy boots, liked trucks, was just starting to severely restrict her own eating, and wanted to be cool. She wanted to see the Dead but her mother was afraid. It was 16 years after my first show and only a few since my last. "I'll go," I offered. "Let me show you the way." The three of us drove up rte 89 to just shy of the Canadian border. When we arrived, the daughter froze. "I don't feel cool," she said. "Relax," I told her. "All these fine people are friends. Smile. You're at the show. You're cool." A couple walked by chanting "1 for 5, 2 for 8, 3 for 10." My advisor repeated it and looked at me. "If you don't know what they're saying, they're not talking to you," I said. It's not an ATM. Smile with a slight polite head shake. We smiled and danced and smiled and sang along for hours. I left my Birkenstocks out on the field. We snacked in the lot for the first hour of traffic. When we got tired we pulled off into the woods and slept all snuggled up in the sports car. I got ice cream in town the next day. The server wasn't happy. He messed up some lyrics to U.S. Blues, he said. "Maybe," I replied, "but it was a damn fine 'Uncle John's Band.'" He relaxed a bit. "Oh yeah, 'Uncle John's Band,'" he said. Our hands grazed around the cone. The song spooled out in our minds, I could see it. The music lives on.

GRATEFUL BY ANN SANCHEZ

I took my first plane ride at the age of 35.
I literally left Texas on the 4th day of July.
I did it to see John Mayer
on the big screen at The Sphere.
I was "miracled" a Ticket by a couple of friends.
I couldn't be more grateful.
With a 7/10 birthday, a show like that is special.
I'd never been to Vegas.
The glitz and glam don't appeal to me, but for a show like that,
 it was worth the experience of what I did see.

The visual effects were like an interactive art display
that gave one euphoria without the high.
Like the cat that tries to chase the red dot,
you can not look at one place for too long.
It's the movie I'd like to watch on repeat,
but every show was different.
I was happy with just the one.

Folsom Field in Boulder,
five years prior, was my first "Dead" show.
Also my first time in Colorado.
Two night shows,
a few days before my birthday.
A time I'll never forget.
First night was the infamous hail storm during, "Cold Rain and Snow."
Second night included more of my favorites.

I wouldn't be a Deadhead
if it wasn't for my love of John Mayer.
I've always been a fan of skulls and roses.
Maybe it was just meant to be.
I'm a brown-eyed woman whose not like other girls.

FIRST TIME DEAD BY BECKY BISHOP WHITE

We walked a few Berkeley streets

to Keystone.
You were the Deadhead,
definitely in the zone.
And I felt alone,

the only one in the sweaty, crowded room
who didn't get it: the tunes,
all that boom-itty boom,
the discordant sounds seemed off-key.
Or was it heartache --
something wrong with me?
I thought I might be in love with you,
and you loved the music,
so why was I feeling sick?
Must be this pulsing heat.
Whatever it meant,
I craved an escape to University Ave,
back on cool pavement.
Even if also choked by smoke
from ciggies and joints,
it would be better than inside.
My East Coast viewpoints
were formed by The British Invasion
and Greenwich Village Folk.
You will eventually see through me
and think I'm a joke.
and I will never see you again.
I stood up to leave.
And then
that's when

Jerry came out with Merl Saunders and they played "Keepers."
My ears opened, my heart swelled; I could dig these seekers

of this incredible, almost edible sound.
I ate it up, that night, like manna, like bread,
when I opened my ears and my heart to The Dead.

THE FIRST SHOW: JULY 4TH, 1990 BY DON MCIVER

Hot.
It had been a particularly dry summer.
George H.W. Bush had busted
all the head shops
on interstate trafficking laws.
No papers, no pipes, no bongs to be had,
so we ventured into a hardware store,
bought a vase,
    cork sealer,
    black electrical tape,
    a brass fitting, filter, and flexible tube
    and built a bong.
All we needed to do was buy some pot,
but, like I said, it had been a particularly dry summer.
So we ventured east
to Bonner Springs, Kansas
to see the Grateful Dead anyway.

At set break, I went left; our seats were right.
I'd got turned around and walked right out of the show.
There was no return.
Hot.
Clear air.
Those stars,
and, "I got these walking blues."

The band started "Scarlet Begonias,"
but I didn't know that song.
Outside, not inside, I finally registered Jerry's plaintive wail:
    "Long distance runner, what you standin' there for?
    Get up, get up, get out of the door…"

Time, fluid now,
I'd lost track of words and how they're used,
so when I tried to walk by the security guard at the gate,
he stopped me.
"You can't go back, and you can't stand still."

No reason, so he finally did
what comes too easily to people
who work security
        and popped me in the face.

I ventured away from the gate
and into a sea of recklessly painted school buses.
I was not okay, and my consciousness...held together
by the swirling pain emanating from my recently clocked nose.
"Well, my heads a splinting, and I'm floating to sound."

An older woman took my hand and escorted me up three short steps
to a remodeled, comfortable bus with tapestries covering the windows
        and throw pillows for chairs.

She sat me down and put a fresh grilled cheese in my hand.
"It all rolls into one/ and nothing comes for free."

Other than the two guys I traveled with,
I knew exactly one person in Kansas.

I disassociated and wandered into the parking lot full of cars but devoid of people,
I followed my eyes into the stars,
the milky way,
and saw the spiral arm and our small place in it
and I was nothing,
had always been nothing
and to nothing I'd eventually return.

Returning, the parking lot, in Kansas, and she appeared.
Spinning in the spiral arm, I saw her in front of me.
"Are you okay?"
I was but wasn't. I returned to my body,
"Hello baby, I'm gone goodbye."

She followed me to my car
and then drifted away and into the show.
I started soaring again.
"Wave that flag, wave it wide and high
"Summertime done come and gone my, oh, my."
No part of me was me.
The whole evening…a collection of songs I still hear.

ODE TO THE DEAD BY ROARSHOCK

O, colors shifting, waves rippling
Wind blowing, rain falling
& music playing.
First, tune up strum cords
Growing volume of sounds
Drums & piano & Always
Guitars. 3 guitars weaving
Together & jamming!
O, Music! O, Colors!
O, bright sun above!
Wine flowing, herbs burning
Faces contorting in streaming
Beaming ecstasy dreaming.
Living! O, living. Music singing!
Singing love songs, work
Songs, bad man's songs, my
Songs and your songs.
Giving songs to people
Who grow happy &
Peaceful in the web.
Loving, moving, smoothly
Dancing. O, dancing!
Like waves of grain
Or wind, or sea
Ripples of human beings
Vibrant allowable moving
Consciousness' expanding
Eyes sparkling, lips parting
Faces shining. O, Life!
O, Dead defy the dead
Proclaim the Living!
O, Dead the music singing!
Waves of music, waves of joy
Surround us. Abound within us.
Cool drops of water
Touch our skin.

It looks like
Rain. It feels like Rain
It must be Rain. O, Rain!
Feel the Music, feel the Rain!
The Dead
Proclaim the Living!
The Laughing. The Loving.
O, we are the Living. Dead
Proclaim the Living!
In music singing words
Poetry playing. O, Joy!
O, beauty, wind, rain, waves
& waves & waves of people.
Sighing friends of common souls.
Enemies of common foes.

Anger freezes.
Living, breathing.
Feeling cool spring breezes.
O, Dead
Proclaim the living!

(After Spartan Stadium, San Jose, California, April 22, 1979)

MY BROTHER, WHO I ONLY SEE AT DEAD SHOWS BY PW COVINGTON

I only see my brother at Dead shows
He's been out of the hospital now,
Five years...maybe more

We always meet up
Way in the back,
At the top of the bleachers,
Or on the amphitheater lawn

Where few people are
Or where those there are, are altered
Because there's always been something
A little altered
A little awkward
About my brother

And the only place I've
Ever seen him truly happy
Is a Dead show

So, every year
We meet up
Summer or Fall
Sometimes in Boulder
Sometimes at Bethel
Sometimes out by the Bay

And we talk
Of superficial things
And share a jay
Catch up, in our way

As Bob Weir's face
Whiskered as Bobby the White
Beams from the Jumboscreens,
And glows over the pit

My brother's
Easy-dancing tie dye smile
Reminds me...it reminds me...

First published in the UK by Coin-Operated Press, in their 'Subcultures' edition.
Written in the stands of Folsom Field during intermission at Dead & Company's Boulder show June 18, 2022.

TRANSFORMATION INVITATION BY RENEE CHANDLER

Feeling the blooming rush
Building up inside
That aching longing
The sacred fire beginning to burn

The rise of collective energy
Circling around me, encouraging
Propelling me inward, somehow upward

The beats form primal urges
And my hungry hips
Slowly start to sway

There's a brilliant tension
As I find my groove
Within the swelling melodies

A cult classic
This family of heads
The love of this music
The rich history that connects us

With each word that we sing
Allowing peace to reign within
No more no less

Meeting on this dance floor
Sometimes an old church
Sometimes a tiny bar
The tunes of the Dead transcend

Opening fresh possibilities
The challenges of the world
Slowly drop from my shoulders
All the strife and fear dissipate

The golden notes slide over us
Welcoming the freedom that they bring
Drenched in clinging sweat
I can feel myself slipping

Slipping into infinity
I have become whole again
As the music carries me
Carries me home

SWEET DEAD HAIKUS BY CHUCK TAYLOR

The music pulses
on like Indian ragas.
Life lasts forever.

      Microphones lift to
      the dark sky, catching each note
      sacred to our ears.

Dancers spin and stretch
on the grass hoping to reach
into ecstasy

      I lean against a
      chain-link fence smoking a joint.
      Let everyone in!

Jerry Garcia's
face glows to show a full plate
of ultimate joy

      You may say I'm a
      dreamer, but no, peace and love
      do find a home here

STONED BY KEN GOODMAN

GodSun clean through
mind-moonlit zone
is opposite of far, for
it kisses where it's caught
in/as [this] enskulled star—
casting deLight through
              mind lampshade(s)
where the gravestones are.

HIGH IDENTITY BY KEN GOODMAN

Zero name for *I AM*
equals high identity:
egoless deity;
way to find it vanishes
       upon discovery.

PSILOCYBIC SEXUAL MICROGRAVITY BY NANCY PATRICE DAVENPORT

the smallest speck
floats in this space
it's a dark void
alone and a lonely
time bends
Time floats   time stretches
time suspends

dark star crashes

I bend
I float
I stretch

afloat in portals
a cosmic dust mote   shining gold

reason tatters

sound is amplified
I take endless showers
in amniotic fluid
and ash

then there's the peaceful reconciliation:

I'm naked
I'm dripping   awaiting rebirth

TO THE MEN I MET AT A DEAD SHOW IN 1981 BY LEAH MUELLER

We tried to walk barefoot
into a blizzard, but the security guard
stopped us: an aged elf,
dressed in a lime-green, three-piece

polyester suit that undulated
beneath the fluorescent lights
of the Dane County Colosseum.

The acid had already peaked,
but all of us were still tripping:
thousands of freaks in sweaty tie-dyed
shirts, swirling and hugging, waving
our arms like trees in a windstorm.

You and I met at the concert,
jogged in place to "Bertha",
and decided to stroll outdoors
for a breath of ice-cold air.

"I can't let you out," the guard said.
"It's against the rules."

The concept of rules at a Dead show
struck us as funny, so we laughed
for what felt like a long time.

You asked "Why?"
and the guard looked dejected,
like he really wanted to let us
play barefoot in snowdrifts,
but would face harsh punishment if he did.

"I just can't," he replied.
"Besides, you don't have any shoes on,
and, well, it's snowing."

I gazed down at your feet,
pale and knobby with bulging red veins,
and laughed harder, while the guard
waited patiently for me to stop.

Finally, I met his eyes.
A tiny bee sticker made from cloth
was affixed to the lapel of his green suit.
The bee was smiling.

"I like that," I said. "It's cute."
"I'm glad," he replied.
"Do you want one?"

Reaching into a pocket, he extracted
an entire roll of cloth bugs—
butterflies, caterpillars, dragonflies,
every insect imaginable, marching in circles
around the circumference,

and I said, "Yes, please,"
as I selected a ladybug for my shirt.

He disarmed us without firing
a single shot, so we had no choice
but to wander back into the auditorium,
where "Bertha" was still playing.

We hadn't missed a note.

ALMOST FOUR P.M. BY B. ELIZABETH BECK

On my treehouse balcony, drunk
on oxygen and Bloody Marys
after hours manicuring gardens.
Sweep, prune, weed, clean out
garage, tossing into garbage
what no longer serves, child gone.

Listening to jazz, pups lie
at feet, wind sweeps through
branches of sugar maple
while goose circles, lonely
without his mate as my brother
meets my mother to plant
flowers too early, but I
remain silent still, playing
the long game as Grateful Dead
cues up "Friend of the Devil,"

no coincidence, reconciliation
of light and dark, I withdraw
within contentment. Don't
all animals crave comfort?

Yet still/always/never naïve
enough/betrayed too often,
jaded, hurt, still seeking
joy within notes filling spaces
between breezes and bird calls.
Sapphire ring cased in gold
on finger that binds my heart
beyond love I seek on the pond

beyond this balcony moment.
I forgot this. Think time slides
by so quickly until I'm reminded
of new cycle yet again. It's the winds.

Why my heart soars after such
destruction, I don't know. Masochism.

No, wait. Natural self-destruction
delights, charms even as I'm shocked
and dismayed by upheaval yet rejoice,
craving to carve a poem on the page
as "Fluffhead" cues up, dog of same
name wanders out. Branches

of sugar maple lady mock, enticing
anticipation, only completely,
not quite. Bare branches, last
to open, first to fall. Price

to pay for such majesty. I,
self-proclaimed worshipper
of trees, impatiently patient
wait for her to answer
vernal equinox call to life,
as I focus on face of sapphire
reflecting branches in mini-
composition of everything
contained in one space between
notes that soar as I trust

the pace of life as breath

as much as I trust next note
soaring my soul beyond. Not
whispering winds, but Aries
energy fuels gusts, making
chimes ring, so many strands
I bead, place, set, string
from branches to sing
in accordance to the gold

I weave around wrists.
Look up, spot kids on
neon green kayaks paddling
surface, diamond dappled
like Cave Run Saturdays
I grieve when boat towed.

Yet another mark/clearing/
shift of season I crave
privacy to accept/embrace.
No call to lose time
layering beats on drum today.
Too busy gulping moments,
evoking yoga breath
that launched/catapulted
energy into present. Yet another

brick in time, stacking against
what plagued memories Friday,
April cool melancholy
overcoming senses I accept
quietly, grateful to shroud
silence, isolation in response.
Recourse not reactionary.

AURORA BOREALIS LADY BY NANCY PATRICE DAVENPORT

everything good must end, she says
beautiful Gemini
geomagnetic radiation and psilocybin create
a tie-dyed purple sky tonight

it's breathing

we lie on our backs to watch

all the years combine
they melt into a dream

this connection reaches across years

decades, really

we are broken angels flying crooked

your eyes look like shot silk:
lavender to navy
the shade of the sky at dawn
or just past dusk

you are my past,
you are my present

some things are simply eternal

in the end there's just the song

SET ON THE DEAD BY JIM LANDWEHR

Growing up, I never was much of a Dead fan
to me they and their music seemed aimless and
wandering.

The switch came when I heard them while high
might have been a doobie or pipe hits, I don't
remember.

It was their Dead Set album live from 'frisco
that pulled me in and became a repeat
listen.

Suddenly their music made complete sense
the way it seemed to take its time, what's the rush
anyway?

Jerry's voice on one song, Bob Weir the next
trading guitar riffs and solos with mutual
respect.

The dual drummers thumping their relevance
while the squeaky Hammond shrieks its
entrance.

All of it held together by the backbeat
of the bass player steady and reliably
present.

But it was at their concert at Alpine Valley
in '87 that made the deal go down for this Dead
skeptic.

Over two hours of winding guitar solos,
vocal harmonies, peace, love, happiness, and
smoke.

I don't mean to advocate for illegal drug use
but for me it gave life to a band I thought was
Dead.

NEVER MISS A SUNDAY SHOW BY J. MARTIN STRANGEWEATHER

In the wilderness
The music
Is the sound
Of the noise

The ecstasy
Of flailing my wild hair on a sweaty Sunday night
In the transdimensional temple of dancing lights
Where God expands in sonic fractals
Melting all our nomadic brains into a single mind
Radiating chemical mandala halo
While rosy-eyed angels gracefully twirl with devilish grins

In the city
The noise
Is the sound
Of the music

The irony
Of standing in line at the DMV early Monday morning
Next to a skeletal skinhead skag addict
Enveloped in prison tattoos that draw my attention
Away from his boldly missing teeth
Going on about the purity of his bloodline
And the greatness of his ancestors

In the elevator
The sound
Is the noise
Of the Muzak

The absurdity
Of stepping back into the workaday scheme
While the aftereffects of a weekend on Mars still linger
Sitting in eggshell white cubicle confinement, because
Whether the medium of exchange

Is based on sheep or gold or overinflated promises
It's our very lives we're bartering

DEAD POEM BY SCOT GRESHAM-LANCASTER

In the Cow Palace 1974, the lobby spun,
Floor swirled, pulsed, anticipation begun,
Owsley Orange barrel coming on
The Wall of Sound waited for us all
Waves of fervor surged, pushing tight,
Against the exit doors,
our path in sight.

An unseen hand moved the mindful throng,
Guiding us where echoes once belonged,
Into a space where grandeur sprawled,

The Wall of Sound began,
enthralled us
A Dark Star fell from the Carousel's might,
A ballroom lost in years of shimmering light,
Ears and eyes, ensnared in the dream,
No exit sign, no final scheme
Third eye blinking...

Hypnotic whirl, a spectral tease,
Assured us of the mystic's ease,
In that shaman's realm
where the soul's embrace,
It took us deep,
 lost in grace.
Together

We all remember

GLEN FALLS, '79 BY MARGARET R SÁRACO

I was there

You're a dire wolf
in the promised land
looking for Cassidy,
but you're headed to El Paso,
loser, where Peggy-O still waits
for you singing
Minglewood Blues.
Are you easy to love?
Althea would say no.
You're a lost sailor,
and a saint of circumstance.
Deal me in on Shakedown Street,
yours, the greatest story ever told.

Sometimes I wonder if I have boarded
the same ship of fools as you,
with eyes of the world open
in case the estimated prophet
makes an appearance.

Then, as the drums do not fade away
we'd see if Black Peter is nearby.
Don't you go around and around?
Hours of music, pot, and acid
will take us both far away.

FULL MOON ON HAMPTON BEACH BY TOMMY TWILITE

Casino Ballroom tonight of all nights
Ratdog knows
"Good music can make sad times better"
The dead move on
no longer grateful but at peace
Blackbird eyes
are all I see
no need to cry
because the kid has an ace
up his sleeve
but I was a day late
and a dollar short
to see the show

I was there though
at Umass in '79
on what would someday be
my wedding anniversary
when Pav Smith fell off the stage
well almost
and the Dead swirling
Stag-o-lee
like flowers in the sun
with 40 grand on the field
and sweet, sweet sunshine before the rain
as me and TimO scaled the ladder to the press box
higher than the full moon in May
and opened the trapdoor to say hey to the Chief
who said and I quote:
"Get the fuck out of here you two fucking idiots!"
So beautiful...shining out
like a song

GRATEFUL: DEAD OR ALIVE BY JOE KIDD

you stood there before us as we stared at the sun
hearts taking their time
we had no idea where we were, where did you go
who was that dark man from the red planet
every chord every note every beat every color
bled and you know what blood can do
plug in plug into the light
we searched for the alien the alien harmony
others were calling you "the best of"
something we ran out of
we ran out of our minds
right there in your presence we dropped
dropped with the dead and we never returned
purple chocolate moving in our mouths
we could have had anything, we settled for all of it
but we couldn't take it with us because we were the dead

sometimes occasionally you know it rained inside
the theater of unreal non existent sometimes
border less southern we slept on the river
flowing ducking drinking the vibrant departed
oooohh
you are how many of you are there are there here
but wait it is possible it could happen
walls shake and tremble and splash your thunderous roar
lion may I recall you when I play when I recall the colors of that world
the normal the real the them could never hear you
crawling on all floors they fell asleep but did not dream in color

did we dream you do the angels dream dance kiss drop
don't worry love is not a liar you live in eternity electric

disappear and stay forever
disappear and stay forever

PORTRAIT OF A DESERT CONCERT BY JON LAWRENCE

After *"Black Peter"*

This canyon wind,
pocketful of gust
slipping through the gorge.

Bushes stiff as new bristles,
this pink dusk river dust
in my throat, gritty desert lozenge.

While sand boulders up my nose
My best friend Greg places
his sunburnt arm around me

and says *we've found the hidden
valley:* all river sparkles & pontoon
sliced sunlight. So many strangers

in desert's handshake, heatwave harassment,
sunhat serenade. There's Sergio,
beard tangled like mangroves, says

It's been hot for seven weeks now,
& passes his joint with closed eyes.
There's Old Man Chris, a bubble gum

wrapper acid smuggler, The Awning Boys
selling free shade, Body Spritzers so no one
dries out, Cooler Corrals where the ice

is baptized, all of us bleeding sweat
in unison while the band plays,
when a face I don't know

can nod to a guitar bend and I can
now die in this desert, hold its dirt fingers,
hold everyone even when the heat

reeks across the plain,
when our bodies are the trees
uprooted in dusty stampede.

DANCE (DEAD SHOW) BY TRISH HOPKINSON

A forest of voices
A field of flowers
One hundred thousand
Yes– we're all brothers and sisters,

inside our heads
a drum roll please.
Madmen and their souls–
dancing, dancing.

Dancing, to the living, loving
notes of a guitar and a voice.
The song has no motive,
not a thought of time,

not an hourglass in the audience.
Simply, a break from reality,
a door into ecstasy, no locks,
no keys, no burdens.

And me, I can soar.
I can fly. I need no wings.
The song he sings is a tribute to us.
They say the world is a stage.

Some strive to perform,
the other ones, they dance.
Let your long hair down.
Let your dirty bare feet,

let them dance.

THE NIGHT I HEARD A NEW DEAD SONG BY ECKHARD GERDES
I was at a show near Chicago —
I can't remember when —
Time is an artificial construct, anyway.
The place was patrolled by police.
I think they were off-duty Chicago PD.
We were all uncomfortable.
This was the same place I'd seen
someone crack an empty fifth across the face of an Andy Frain
at a Rolling Stones show
only a couple of weeks earlier.
Now the crowd surged forward,
perhaps to escape the discomfort,
but that Led to a crush.
Fans in front were being pushed
Into the stage, and those behind
were also being squeezed in turn.
In response, the band announced
a new song and began to play,
"One, two, three...take a step back....
One, two, three...take another step back...."
Crowd dancers sensed the movement
and spun back away from the stage.
This had never been meant to be a spectacle,
and had always been meant to be a dance.

THAT WILL CHANGE TODAY BY ROLANDO SERNA

I often wonder
are there certain
requirements
to be,
to become,
to remain
a deadhead?

Have I attended enough shows?
Is it too late?
Do I have to have a
Bob Weir, Phil Lesh, Mickey Hart
encounter story?
Jerry no longer being an option.

Does it count
if I only get to enjoy
The Grateful Dead
on the weekends while fishing in Port Mansfield,
cruising on my electric wheelchair
at the Alamo Texas flea market
on my iPhone Bluetooth
to my hearing aids,
eating locally grown fruits
drinking freshly squeezed lemonade
from an *aguas frescas* glass container
listening to "Uncle John's Band"
on my phone's highest volume setting,
drowning out the local live band,
enjoying my time alone?

Remembering that during
COVID the flea market was
a dangerous place to be for most,
for me and my daughter
it was the place where we sold masks

for financial survival while
listening to the Grateful Dead.

I love hearing that, my friends
continued going to shows.
Reading their posts and seeing the pictures
has always put a smile on my face.
I am happy for them.

I know that I will always be
a deadhead and it saddens me
to know that there will be
generations of kids

who never went to a
Grateful Dead concert
with their parents.

No longer will people meet,
see
a dancing bear
that says,
"It's ok,
I know we have not met.
That will change today."

The bears
let you know:
"Yes, I am kind.
I know you are too."

DEADHEADS : AN ERASURE POEM BY SUSAN BEALL SUMMERS

Jerry Garcia Interview with Christopher Hazard October 13, 1989

      A large part of my life
something way more fun
places I never imagined.
a cultural artifact
slow continuous success
         a surprise, a left field thing

      deadheads
all shapes and sizes and forms
street people
solid professionals
Capitol Hill
they've permeated society
        they are mainstream

      they've invented us:
there's a mutual thing happening
experience is rewarding
celebrate their existence

      a record is like a painting
study all the detail
playing live is like a polaroid
        the moment provides new things

      Built to Last
a million times better
more interesting than conventional success
      I'm happy

UN-DEAD BY SUSAN BEALL SUMMERS

I've never been Dead,
not really.

Held down by being good,
electrocuted with archaic rules,
drowned by hypocritical morality.

Religion took it's course:

small town with few outlets for rebel spirits
Lord Calvert and bonfires by the river
had their own dogma

As far from Haight-Ashbury
as Atlantic to Pacific—
yet waters and cultures mingle in the middle

Dead music was a conveyance
from the out-there to the heart rhythms
started in the 70s all across America
As peace and true personal expression.

RADIO SAINTS BY DOUG D'ELIA

The moment the song "Terrapin Station"
came on the dashboard radio
I knew I wouldn't leave my car
until it had finished playing.

What's 16 minutes and 23 seconds
in my life anyway, measured against the risk
of unnerving Saint Cecelia,
the patron saint of music?

And if my friends don't want to sing
along with me, they can get out of the car
or sit quietly looking out the window
at the cawing sea gulls,

darting in and out of sea foam,
their web feet scratching the sand
like a needle hurrying across
a well-worn record.

AFTER LISTENING TO GRATEFUL DEAD SONGS AT 4 AM BY JOHANNA ELY

Hey, Uncle John,
those first days were the sweetest days—
sugar magnolias in bloom by the river,
lovers walking in splintered sunlight,
deep kisses tasting of summer wine.
We had everything delightful,
crazy tie-dyed dreams to follow—
C'mon, honey. Come along with me.

The crow still tells your stories—
memories and melodies carried
on the morning breeze,
yellow leaves drifting down.
We want to know—
where *did* the time go?

It's a buck dancer's choice
my friend, and we chose Love—
fire over ice.
You played the music,
we danced wildly to your fiddle—
those dreams we dreamed
so long ago
now kept in a box of rain.

Uncle John, we miss you and the band.
We are skeletons who still breathe—
our hands filled with faded red roses.
We ask every angel we meet,
Are you kind?
Have you come to take us home?

SUSPENSION BY B. ELIZABETH BECK

After "Box of Rain"

He lies in bed, half-
sleeping, listening
to the Grateful Dead
I blast through speakers

I know it's only months
before he leaves again
and wonder what he
will remember

and what he will forget
and wish there was a way
to freeze a moment
without stopping time

WOMEN OF LONG MEMORY BY TED MCCARTHY

Walk out any doorway
waiting on the wind
to blow back yesterday's ashes
so fine the skin can't feel.
Only the eyes smarting
under an ineffectual sun
witness the invisible,
and the old signs,
Victualler, Emporium, will be
the last of the street to fall.

There is always another town
or the same maybe, at an hour
when first walkers lace up,
ready to venture in and out
of fog where approaching shapes
solidify. It comes and goes
as if under an enchantment
but is never more
than a trick, a buzzing in the head,
an unpinned disquiet.

Reluctant as a child
they went, those women
of long memory who swept paths
along the width of their front walls,
whose rituals were a lamp
before household gods.
They worshipped a sun
that rarely showed, the earth
in their bodies took them, laid them
to be brushed by strangers.

Theirs the breath you long for
on your face when you step
onto a pavement littered
with droppings and gum, under
brackets for redundant awnings;
a strong hand on a hot
and dusty road, turning toward
that far hill you heard of
at someone's knee, her voice
taller than a spire.

WALK OUT OF ANY DOORWAY BY NANCY SOBANIK

While strains of Bob and Jerry stir my brain,
outside my window lies a crate of snow.
As Phil and Robert fill a *Box of Rain*,
onslaught that carved the gap begins to slow.
The splat and plink of sleet against the pane
replaced with calm; sweet hush to softly grow.
This trailer's mounded high, a hobbit hill.
Inside the empties lie amongst the chill.

Lethargic dormancy of dreams in gray
belied as morning's star gleams bright as brass.
Bejeweled and ermine-cloaked the balsams sway
and soon the plows will open wide the pass.
The blizzard spent, I'll exit from the fray;
for doors that keep me caged are only glass.
I'll cross the threshold, walk out through that door;
leave the crate, it's just a crate and nothing more.

After The Grateful Dead "Box of Rain," American Beauty
Written in a Double Ottava Rima scheme- a form of poetry consisting of stanzas of eight lines of ten or eleven syllables, rhyming abababcc.

PHONE CALL FROM MY NEPHEW BY ROBERT COOPERMAN

We rave about the Nuggets,
kvelling like proud parents over
their darling's Nobel Prize:
Denver finally the NBA champs.

Then he mentions his crappy work week
and how he needed to get away,
so he and his girlfriend caught
The Dead and Company on their farewell tour.

"Played all our favorites,
and played them great," Alby chuckles,
still hearing the music in his head.
"If not for you," he goes on, "I'd never
have known about the Dead,
when you took me to that outdoor concert
 the year after Jerry died."

"I remember. We'd brought an extra
rain slicker for you, but didn't have one
for your friend, so you shared.
When the monsoon hit, man, you two
looked like drowned rats, so we left,
to avoid getting electrocuted,
like the Dead almost did at Woodstock."

But Alby wasn't even born then,
and I never attended: my cousin's wedding
that weekend; I wouldn't have missed it
for anything, especially if I'd known
how short a time Larry had left,

though if there is a heaven
I hope the Dead will play set after set
for my beautiful cousin.

THE BASEBALL CAP BY ROBERT COOPERMAN

We order at the sub shop's counter,
and instead of asking for my name,
the guy smiles,

"We'll send it right out, Bob."

"How...?" I start, but he interrupts:

"Your Grateful Dead baseball cap,
I remember it from the last time
you and your wife were in."

I want to quip something
a fellow Deadhead would get,
but settle for, "Thanks, Man,"
and hobble back to our table
with a tad more swagger
than my cane usually allows:

I think about the Sphinx's riddle
about what goes on four legs
in the morning (an infant),
two at noon (a grown man),
and three (an old man with a cane)
at dusk, that only doomed Oedipus
could answer.

So now, Beth and I wait for our subs:
impatient for the delicious crunch
of the first toasted bite,
sort of like our anticipation
of the Dead's two drummers
hitting the downbeat
of the show's opening number,

when we'd dance all night.

VISITING FRIENDS IN ATHENS, GEORGIA BY ROBERT COOPERMAN

Hugh and I sit on his deck
in the cool of a late May afternoon,
and the topic turns to music.

"What's your favorite story-song?"
he asks, and I tell him "Jack Straw,"
which he's never heard of, then add,

"You do know I can turn any conversation
into a lecture on the Grateful Dead,"
and he gives me that small, knowing laugh
of having fed me a hanging curve:

Two desperadoes up-to-no-good,
in the late 19th century West,
one lagging farther and farther behind,
maybe shot in a robbery they escaped from
with some loose change and a few cheap rings.

At the end, Jack Straw digs a shallow grave
for his "old buddy" he may or may not
have fatally shot, impatient the poor bastard
was "moving much too slow."

"The Dead," I tell him, "loved
to sing about bank and train robbers,
bootleggers, loser-poker players and card sharps,
bigamists on the run, helped by their friend,
the Devil: their world a rogue's gallery of stories."

Songs of young forever-love
under moons in June?
Too many of those already.

SECOND VISIT TO THE AUDIOLOGIST'S OFFICE BY ROBERT COOPERMAN

Since he said he liked poetry,
I dropped off one of mine for him,
Saved by the Dead,
which he thought would be a delving
into the world of kindly spirits.

"But I should've known from your t-shirt,"
he smirks, "this was about the Grateful Dead."

Then he shows me how to fit
these hearing aids into my ears,
though I have about as much dexterity,
with my bum right hand, as a starfish.

I show him my right wrist, savaged
in an accident when I was a kid,
and he whistles.

"You're lucky to be here."

Lucky too that I can hear
with carillon clarity
the songs that made the Dead
love-at-first-listen.

FRIEND OF THE DEVIL BY B. ELIZABETH BECK

Bathed in blue light, she sings
tunes so sweet, Jerry smiles, roses

bloom in magical halos
in this tiny local bar, spirit

of Grateful Dead found best
in tribute musicians capture

energy spun, never fades
away from our hearts, souls

ache as bodies dance, strangers
stop strangers a bit older now

yet still connected when band
takes the stage and first note

launched, excitement blossoms
recognizing familiar songs, anthem

of our youth, lifestyle one miracle
encased in tie dyes, spinning

rainbows from crystals, scarlet
begonias wither as bones creak

yet hearts beat together, path
is for our steps when no pebble

is thrown, no wind to blow.

BLUE PYRAMID BY ROARSHOCK

Blue moon evening
in a blue room
barely autumn
quietly drifting along
into winter.

I see a month gone
and a full moon
electric frenzy
'neath the Blue Pyramid.

Gleaming in the hieroglyphic dark
mysteries so far away
from all that we know.

Sphinx images.
Lions in the night.
Lines of darkness.

Greatly moved
'neath your moon and your stars
but in what night desert
stands that Blue Pyramid...

There is yet more to tell
for this is no museum
in which hangs
a tapestry of words
that the desert sands
blow through.

Seek not to solve the mystery.
Relax
in the desert night.

GRATEFUL KU BY JOHN SAVOIE

my dark star
you bend the space
around you
*

redwood grove
shafts of light
touching earth
*

evening sweeps
the splintered sunlight
yellow moon
*

broken shell
the color of sky
this bird has flown
*

notch-wing crow
wheels and dips
the fountain's mist
*

splasshhh . . .
I get up to find the moon
rippling the pond
*

pennies
in the dust
a dime
*

hotel by the hump yard
all through the night
banshees cry
*

clockwise cat
asleep on the couch
time pauses
*

dusty frets
one string sprung
attic hush
*

tattered rope
rusted pulley
bucket gone
*

headlights shine
through the cool
Colorado rain
*

these dreams
walking barefoot
in snow
*

how quick
the cup
grows cold
*

how slow
the empty cup
fills with light
*

laryngitis
more and more
I just smile
*

rising tide
time for this one
to go home

EVERY DAY BY PATRICIA J. DORANTES

Every single day I flow with the wind,
Freely, without fear of tomorrow.
My mind is untangled from limits,
There is nothing to fear anymore.
I am not alone with my mind anymore,
As I vibrate to your same wavelength.
Sound flows thru my thin blood veins,
Divine thunder that shakes cold hearts.
Every single day my vision keeps changing,
From the barn to the skyscrapers there's wonder,
You and me, we are different, yet the same.
Sometimes, I do fear the crawling darkness,
But the kaleidoscopic whispers keep me company,
Telling me everything is going to be all fine.

A SWEET STAB TO MY HEART BY MOORE NGWENYA

The vibration of the bass, harp,
cymbals and violin strings.
Producing tonnes of energy.
Pumping energy to my heart.
Invigorating it to beat day to day
A sweet stab to my heart

It circulates my body
Running through my veins.
As the pitch Pierce's my heart.
Sending waves of relaxation through my limbs.
Making me move to every beat.
As my feet taps to every drum
Bang.
While my fingers snap at the relieving tempo.
A sweet stab to my heart.

Killing my ears with waves of softness.
Reprocessing the feelings reigning the moment.
Discarding all silence into voices of a song.
Bringing me back from the world of despair
and emotional emptiness.
Flying me through timelines of artists of music growth.
Growling different artists into recording song disc.
Allowing the dagger to deepen onto my sweet stab.
Sending emotions through the words of the
Microphone in the studio.
Bleeding a fame of elation to the roaring fans

MUSIC IN THE PARKING LOT BY EMECHETA CHRISTIAN

In the shimmering heat of summer '89,
I found redemption between painted Volkswagen vans,
where rainbow-haired prophets traded miracles
like baseball cards, and patchouli danced with cleverness
through curtains of forests hung between makeshift cities.

The first notes of "China Cat Sunflower"
rippled through the crowd like electric honey,
and Jerry's guitar spoke in tongues
that even the angels had forgotten—
each riff a silver yarn in the cosmic cuddle.

Time became elastic, stretching like taffy
through three-hour jams that felt like minutes,
or maybe centuries. Who could tell
when Phil's bass lines were rebuilding DNAs
and Bobby's rhythm was teaching atoms new ways to spin?

A girl with eyes like kaleidoscopes
handed me a flower and whispered,
"The music never stopped, it just keeps echoing
through different dimensions." She spoke truth—
I've heard "Dark Star" in meteor showers
and "Sugar Magnolia" in butterfly migrations.

The lot became our Jerusalem,
each tour a pilgrimage to find
that perfect moment when the band
and ten thousand souls breathed as one
through "Morning Dew" or "Friend of the Devil."

Now I catch glimpses of that magic:
in a stranger's tie-dye at the grocery store,
in my daughter humming "Box of Rain,"
in dandelion seeds spinning through sunbeams
like dancers at the Acid Tests.

Some say the Dead were just a band,
but we know better—they were cartographers
mapping the spaces between heartbeats,
mathematicians solving equations
with guitar strings and drum fills,
alchemists turning simple notes
into pure California gold.

And somewhere, in a parallel universe,
that summer night in '89 is still playing,
the music never stopped, never will it stop,
as long as there are ears to hear
and hearts to hold the endless groove.

Every show was a new translation
of the same ancient story:
How rhythm and light and love
can turn strangers into family,
and family into constellations
dancing across the infinite stage
of a parking lot universe.

GUITAR LESSONS BY UZOMAH UGWU

Tempted by his way with words
Gave choruses for the birds to sing

A masked beauty
Hiding in disguise

"Where are you going?"

I saw his words written in
The clouds
"Don't say my name in vain if you go."

His eyes were soaked in the air.

"Never I enjoy why you came."

He grabbed his guitar and picked a song
To lead the way
We stopped by the river for a game of spades
He told me fables
Not found in books

"Is this what you wanted?"

There were things I couldn't say
Not that this was not where I wanted to be
I loved to be with him
Between the moon and sun
Where the river whispered to us

THE CROWD BY UZOMAH UGWU

The crowd knows chords of sorrow
Marches of bands play songs

That leaves the air anew
Attached to soundless emotions

Ghosted by lyrics that
Frame stages of known names

Seeking the one while knowing someone
It is better to love hard than soft to the crowd

Values to the core, sing along
With choirs known in churches

I have sung sonnets labeled
with your name. I tame all types of flames
and to those who love with less and say why they live to love
while all are watching people dance as the music starts with
daring glances. Instead of a brilliant romance

I make and take bets that this was worth it
Even after the curtain call and the crowd left
The music never stopped

I HAVE LIVED BY UZOMAH UGWU

I have lived sad love songs
Played their records
Been lost in their melodies
Their lyrics know my name

I had a childhood that
When I reflect on it
It might turn
My hair grey

I made my bed not to sleep
In it but to keep
Something neat
In my room

I own my depression
Because I can't return
It or let it go

FROM ITS LIFE— IT'S SOULE— IT'S BREATH! BY KATRENIA GRACE BUSCH

This song strung of chords in number seven,
That unite mine tongue to heels—
That in such nature as poetic verse fasten;
To the scythe of crescent moon's harvest that reveals,

Mine heels lifted from below the ground,
That mine— voice be silent as winds held back—
That mine tongue be loosened but to its own end bound,
That speech— be formed from time and time I lack!

Formed from my tongue and womb therein,
That mine feet might know its own—
Divided as mine legs did mine tongue hold myself within—
To measure between what's new and old!

Beneath the moon that grew from light to darkest days—
The sea was found to roar and rise—
Did— mine feet move from two to one with my tongue that weighs,
Upon the scales of libra— mine heart would comprise:

A tune from whistles strung by heavens abode—
From tongue and heels that meet!
Under the poetic moonlit skies they rode,
As pair— together— as feet!

Ah! King Oedipus! Thine understanding wise,
When what's new is old and old is new by time and times and time
    again—
Was mine heart lifted— as its weight in size,
Against— mine feet of tongue and heels of what was and what's been!

Footprints established once afore,
When walked twice by death—
That— this song of poetry sought to pour
From its life— its soule— its breath!

SING A SONG O YESTERDAY! BY KATRENIA GRACE BUSCH

Mine tongue was lifted from its idle grave;
That it might be inclined to sing—
Sing it did from sunset to sunrises which gave—
The moon its light— that mine feet, my footprints clung to dancing!

O yesterday! How yourself did mirror time!
That brought unto itself the scythe of nightfall—
That the crescent of times shaped under the moonshine—
Be counted as days— in number— beneath what's called the all,

Hear mine hearts whispers O yesterday!
That the whistles be made known—
That fiery fowls fly— until found to weigh;
Against— thine time, times— once sown!

O fiery fowls— let yesterday know thine ways!
The fixed hand of the trinity of fate be as stone!
This— I've sought after that I might count our days—
Our days— that be confined to time, time, times alone!

Let this be the decree of time and time again—
Known as yesterday and all that is and will be,
That the hand of fates be thrice spun by times of when—
When— the immortal times live beyond the all eternally!

FARE THEE WELL BY LYNN WHITE

Fare thee well
the dead, undead and undying.
Even when only the bones remain
there's a dance to be danced
and laughs to be had
loud and louder
laughs
playing out
in the music.
Fare thee well
the undying dead.

MARRYING A DEADHEAD BY LISA SCHNAIDT

In loving memory of John Walter Schnaidt 8/4/54-8/2/24

Forty-six years of hearing Jerry and the boys
soon changed into a musical obsession filled with joy.
Tapers, box sets and a favorite '72 show,
I was Dead-ucated and didn't even know.

Collections, must-haves, and a vast Dead library
soon became part of my necessary therapy.
His cancer came out of left field.
Dead music was used to try to heal.

Chemo, pumps, radiation and pills
couldn't defray our Grateful Dead thrills.
Six-hour treatments were beastly to endure
but Grateful Dead Sirius helped as a soul-healing cure.

August 2, 2024 you took your last breath,
and I kept my promise and played "He's Gone"
as you ascended with the Angel of Death.
This Deadhead girl will never forget
the beloved that taught her
via reels, vinyl, CD and cassette.

Rest easy my love and jam on your heavenly drums
the music that filled your soul and all goodness flowed from.
I know you're with Jerry, Pigpen, Keith and Brent
creating music with such incredible talent.
and chatting with Robert Hunter on "What a Long, Strange Trip It's Been"
as I long for the day to see you again.

Be it "Box of Rain," "Black Peter," "Scarlett Begonias" or "Morning Dew,"
"Ripple," "St. Stephen," "Wharf Rat" or "U.S. Blues,"
"Terrapin Station," "Truckin'," "Althea" or "Touch of Grey,"
 you know our love will "Not Fade Away."

GONE BY B. ELIZABETH BECK

"nothing's gonna bring him back" —Robert Hunter

I would rather be driving the wrong way,
wish time could U-turn as easily

as Maralee navigates from Michigan
to Ohio after Soldier Field, Jerry's last

show (we did not yet know) amusing mishap
when merely maps and instincts guided

journeys we considered Odyssean, accepting
calls of Sirens, languishing in Land

of Lotus Eaters, evoking merry pranksters
in our quest to follow pied piper behind

white beard had he not crashed.

Reprinted from *Dancing on the Page* (Rabbit House Press, 2024)

AT MY FUNERAL BY ECKHARD GERDES

At my funeral
play the Dead's "He's Gone."
Dance in a conga line,
laugh and be happy.
I have lived a long, good life,
all-in-all,
and I don't want to be one to whine,
so make it snappy!

I'm off to dance with my wife
in the halls
of where no one's alone,
where we are all fine.
Children, even your pappy
had to heed the fife
and answer the call
to go back home
to the astral plane.

Invite a hippie and a yippie,
but no one with a knife.
Invite the short of cash, one tall,
one artist, and one bum.

One artist? Make it nine—
one for each life, no matter how crappy.
And the time is rife
for riffs and response-and-call—
bring many musicians—at least some,
and break out some wine
and make the day less sappy.

Let them smooth out feelings that are rough
and let the dance arrive.
Laugh and sing and drink till you fall,
and know that you're the poems
of my soul that I carry back whence I came.

BOB THOMAS BY HAKIM

He was a friend of mine.
We used to sit behind the Coffeehouse
and talk about the world
and why it was
how it was.

At first we drank Green Death together and
smoked out of the Bugler pouch.
      He was a good old man,
      spare of body and of words
      except after the appropriate loosening.
      Helluva musician too: made his own pipes
      & some are even in museums
      in European castles & all.

Then sometime later, though I still smoked
cheap tobacco, I matched him
chai for Green Death
drink for drink,
until he was down & plowed, and I was not
because I had to fix my life
& beer seems to not help
a single bit.

      He knew old Owsley, did Bob –
      went *carcelado* for his mate
      back in the day.

I liked the music of the Dead well enough
and I guess Bob didn't mind it too much
but I know in his heart
he wished they'd all get in tune
like I did.

Bob Thomas was a fantastic musician, restorer of ancient bagpipes, and an artist – he painted the very first **'Steal Your Face'** *skull that you now see everywhere uncredited.*

CATS UNDER THE STARS BY SHANNON EDDY

As high school students, we were
anything but patient. Our smoke machine mouths
Forcing the November rain on a mission
with a simple twist. To acquiesce tone into a tunnel.

I hear my father's murmur "Fucking hippies"
As I pulse luminescent one possessed firefly
amongst possessed fireflies thrusting;
a shroom fever chasing Waterfalls.

One woman claimed to taste
Names with a breadbox tongue.
And I'm sorry Kevins but olive
Juice tastes like semen.

The ice-skater twins twirled inside
tie-dyed spindled ringing dusts.
A gather of planetoid sisters and brothers,
who have crashed in laughter.

There were stories acted out.
Strangers who shouldn't have met.
The one in the bucket hat lost his ticket.
Bit husky Gilligan who forget his friend.

They create handshakes out of miss-steps.
Good intentions aside. They'll struggle to strike
enough syllables in a deal for two unfolded boxes.
They'll reconcile after two years time, apart.

August 9, 1995 my father uttered without joy.
Hippie Jesus was dead, caught by the game.
Downtown Providence sent signal flare serenades.
Poured themselves into the second tune silence
candles within candles make as they flick and puff.

Some sat, wrapping the rink , tears danced.
We were lost on a train.

Learning how to control our batons.
Cochrane fell asleep on the ride home.
Anything but patient

GONE FOR GOOD BY HOWARD BROWN

With no small measure of regret, I recall the Spring
of '95. I was ass-deep in the perception of myself
as an up-and-coming, hot-shot Memphis attorney,
convinced I was on my way to bigger and better things.

So, when I heard the Grateful Dead were coming
to town I was torn between work and an almost
insatiable desire to see the show. But in the end, I
procrastinated, letting work win out, telling myself
I'd catch the Dead the next time around.

Only there'd be no next time - because Jerry Garcia died
in August of that year and shortly thereafter the group
was no more. Then came the jarring Sisyphean epiphany
that work is a constant, it never ends. But not so with the Dead,
once they were gone, they were gone for good.

RUMORS OF THE ANCIENT BY RENEE CHANDLER

I'm not contemplating
Power dynamics
Or the position of the moon

I'm just vibrating
Highest frequency
Tuned in to the show

As if on cue, we lifted him
We lifted each other
In rapture and delight

We are infinite
Dancing in shifting worlds
Stunned as each bruised melody
Touches the skin of the song

Echoes of the masters
As Phil's friends
We cherished and lifted

We are tiny warriors
Blinded by the power
Of our own light

(JUST) A BOX OF RAIN BY KEN GOODMAN

Rain in the box
rain out the box,
leave it if you dare—
GodSky/mindcloud
harmony's
        skull giftboxed
                self-aware:
in & out the window
long time
      short mortality...
 timelessly [this] moment
passed on
insight/edgelessly.

SUNDAY DAYDREAM BY D.L. LANG

Swaying in a sea of tie dye,
grass like incense in the wind,

dizzy dancing like a hurricane
floating upon the wings of songs,
as pirates park in the bay,

stowaways singing along,
kaleidoscopic skeletons tango
with grateful grinning bears

tripping upon happiness
as bubbles reach for the stars,
harmony in the haystack

and peace among the people
as our collective dreams embrace
as a halo of roses watches over us all.

Dancing to the Dead is as easy
as the ocean breeze…

All you got to do is feel.

Written on July 21, 2024 at Phil Lesh's last concert at McNears in San Rafael.

WE HAD OUR PHIL BY ECKHARD GERDES

When the world was still new,
we heard that we could catch rain
if the box wasn't rigid ,
if we looked at it wide-eyed
while we all linked elbows together
in dance and music, and in that way
we could not be broken.
I learned that from you,
all while trying to become
someone other than a drone.
You showed us how to claim
the whispering rumble
that filled our bellies
when no other food would do.
When chaos exploded around us,
you kept us steady but moving.
You showed us how to focus
and keep ahold of the musical
tether you threw out to us
no matter how far we had strayed.
 Insufficiently, thank you.

ASYMPTOTE BY SCOT GRESHAM-LANCASTER

The eschatological overreach
  at the end of days
Stretching to touch the
    asymptotic wonder
  just out of reach
   The Joycean thunder word
Echoing up from bottom
   of the wale of song

The crowd pulsing
With the sympathetic
   resonance of gratitude
    The finality of the last song
The tide still wears down
The ancient sea stones
   At the bass of time

At Winterland
In an impulse of
   psychedelic wonder
I had jumped up on stage
  ran between Bob and Jerry
at their mics
   and sat in the empty plush chair
    at the back of the stage

Someone grabbed my arm
  to guide me off stage,
   Gently
   Firmly
  I then looked across at Phil
    Still playing with an impish grin
     a wink for me

I looked to the person
  guiding me
  Off stage
  Bill Graham looked me in the eye

   "That chair was for
   Pigpen's spirit, not you"
   He said with kindness

 Escorted off and out
    the stage right door
I was met by death's incarnation
    the seventh seal
   "After party
   Jack Tarr hotel,
   Room 257"
   with a silky
calm void blank aura

   I didn't go

 The next morning
   An eagle
     or was it a vulture?
Circled high above me
    at the bus stop
   an impish grin
    a wink for me

   On the ground again
   The metaphysical
   Nature of Reality
just on the other side
    Long black veil
   We can almost touch
   We can always almost join
   The asymptotic unknown ...
   Death

THE GHOST SHIP ON THE BAY BY OZ HARDWICK

Fair winds, smiling seas, the skeleton crew
dances sunshine on the shining decks
to melodies like bright birds wheeling,
as the Captain laughs a lanyard of notes
that loops the ship to the furthest shore.

And as we rock on tide and surge,
we feel that pulse in our shaking bones –
the alchemist in the engine room,
distilling rainbows from light and shade,
carving waves out of ballroom silence.

Ripple and rip-tide speak of the deep,
tectonic plates shifting, fault lines resolving,
and beasts rising from old sailors' tales, as
on the shore, windows are flung wide,
and word goes round: Phil is singing.

PHIL'S DEATH BY ROARSHOCK

I saw the social media post this morning
But did not want to believe it was true.
And then the internet exploded
And then it was on the newswires.
Phil Lesh has died.
He was looking frail the last few years
He had profoundly avoided death for decades
survived near fatal disease, a liver transplant
~ God bless you Cody ~
to grace the stage with so many great musicians
and he brought along so many new young players
helped enshrine the Grateful Dead canon
in the world musical songbook where they will remain
so long as there is music and time, the songs will fill the air.
Shows always ended with Phil urging all in the audience
to become organ donors, help save lives.
"Not that anything is ever going to happen to me,
But if it does, I want to be an organ donor."
For almost fifty years now, I have been in the audience
and the Grateful Dead started following me around even before that!
Then, when Jerry died in 1995 the long, strange trip seemed over.
Until my thirty ninth birthday on October 9, 1999
when I went to see Phil and Friends at the Warfield Theatre.
The curtain pulled back and there was Phil singing
"Like a Rolling Stone"
And I was back on the bus
for another twenty-five years of mind expansion and bliss.
I was seventeen years with Jerry and the Grateful Dead
(on the "Jerry Side" or in the "Phil Zone")
but they were original psychedelic years!
I recall one night before the first set
when the band took the stage and everyone in the audience
had their auras stretching across the room
and I was focused (like so many other times)
on telepathic communication with the Grateful Dead
and looked at Bob who smiled and looked away
then I looked at Jerry who shrugged and looked away
then I looked at Phil who looked right back at me

and fiercely flipped me the bird (Ye olde Zoner Salute!)
and brought me humbly right back into my body.
In the Phil and Friends years, I was seldom so psychedelicized
but often just as high, and exchanged smiles with Phil
from the floor to the stage, stage to the floor.
I took my favorite original hippie girlfriend
(who had avoided seeing the Dead all those years)
to a show with Phil and the Quintet at the Berkeley Greek Theatre.
She was hooked from the first notes of his bass
and we were show companions for the next twenty plus years
with many iterations of the Friends in various venues far and near
including many visits to Terrapin Crossroads, our "clubhouse."
All precious times I will never forget and never remotely imagined
when I started on this long, strange trip.
So, now Phil is dead
and that part of the journey is in the past
experience and music that remains in recordings
 "Preserved in amber." as Phil once said.
But it will never again be that excitement
of waiting for the first set
and the thrill of hearing those first bass notes
when he plugged in and tuned up.
What comes next, I don't know
only that the music will remain and go on
I will enjoy and champion it as long as I still live
and when I die, I don't know
endless sleep seems most likely
but if there is an afterlife
and we all end up in heaven
I will be in that company
with friends and family
and Phil will be in the Angel Band.

OCEAN IN THE SKY BY BRUCE FISHER
(Shoreline Amphitheater, 6/4/95)

It was the hippie girl with her oatmeal cookies and laughing baby.
She caught my eye with a smile that could melt a heart of stone,
and with a voice that sung through the ages,
and that I heard long before she spoke.
I bought one of her cookies for fifty cents and took a bite.
"Mm, good," I said.

She smiled back.
Her baby was staring at me, convulsing with laughter,
And his eyes twinkled like crazy fingers of light,
like the eyes of all the world.
"He likes you," she said.

It must have been some unusual variety of oats
or maybe the butter had gone bad,
but not long after eating it,
sitting tenth row just in front of Garcia's amp,
I began feeling peculiar.
It was still well before show time.

I always arrived early for Dead shows,
And The Shoreline was a great place to see them.
I liked taking in as much of the scene as possible,
And today was special, for due to a series
Of unexplained segues in the third dimension,
I was to meet bass player Phil Lesh at intermission
And hopefully get his blessing
for the film I was writing
about The Grateful Dead.

Everyone around me was high although not necessarily by drugs.
Some of course, and apparently,
I had joined the drug induced subculture of happy rogues.
Mostly people around my age or a little older.
There was a peace in their eyes,
and it calmed me just sitting there,
and made me forget how high I was.

There was something more than just ganja in that cookie,
and I began to feel a warmth moving up my spine
and out through the top of my head.
I rose up out of my body higher and higher
until I hit a soft, gelatinous membrane.

Then a voice said,
"You've reached the soft,
Gelatinous membrane."

"Yes, I know," I answered.

"You must let go if you hope to break through."

"What are you, a therapist?
I don't want to break through,"
I said.

"Oh it's too late for that,"
the voice said, then laughed.

I recognized that laugh.
"Laughing baby, is that you?"

I had never been much into the drug scene.
I was a whiskey and beer, blues-loving pseudo-intellectual from LA,
where my musical taste never went much further
than Lynyrd Skynyrd and Aerosmith,
but I was a long way from all that.

I knew now that laughing baby was a doorkeeper,
a fearless guardian to higher states of awareness,
or as Jerry would say, a signpost to new space,
and that we were all expanding
until a point of crystallization
was reached and we remembered
who we were.
It would happen suddenly. Everyone would just stop and say,
  "Hey, it's you! I know you. It's been you all along,"

As I came through the other side of the membrane,
there were great sea creatures, whales, dolphins, giant squids,
hundreds of them, thousands, all swimming in a great ocean in the sky,
not of water, but of ether.
All sea life was leaving the oceans of earth and taking up residence
in the sky where they could escape the pollution of Man,
and all the land creatures were there too, alive on heavenly islands,
and all the animals I had known through the ages,
all were happy and at peace.

This ocean in the sky reverie continued for what seemed to be hours,
but gradually I descended back into my tenth row seat
just as the Boys were tuning for the first song,
and as Jerry strummed the opening chords of "Bertha,"
I knew that ascension was only a seeming absence.

All I remember about the first set
was dancing like some crazy, alien madman
who stumbled into some cosmic tavern,
quenching his thirst on psychedelic beer kegs
after a lifetime of walking
all the infinite deserts of the galaxy

At intermission The Dead's publicist, Dennis Macnally,
gathered a small group of five or six of us,
and we followed him.
Backstage was a laid back family scene
with a video arcade and pinball machines
set up for the kids—a mini Chuck E Cheese—
the smell of hot dogs and grilled cheese
sandwiches like at a Fourth of July Parade.
The laughter of children was everywhere.

I tried not to look at anything too long otherwise I would get lost in it.
In the middle of one of Jerry's solos,
late in the set I realized that baby did something to me,
put a spell on me with his twinkling eyes and jiggling belly.

We arrived at Phil's dressing room.
Laughing baby had been sitting on Macnally's shoulder.

Macnally either didn't notice or didn't care,
which made me wonder if he was in on it,
although I wasn't sure what "it" was.
Phil was eating dinner while a dude was telling him
about some kind of sound technology he'd invented.
Phil listened and asked questions.
I was beginning to really space out,
but their voices calmed me.

I thought the dude said something
like his new device would allow the musicians
to make themselves invisible while playing.
The idea was ridiculous.
What would be the advantage of invisibility?
They talked for about 45 minutes, and there was no time for me
 to tell him about my film after that,
which was good as it gave me time to come down a bit.

"Let's go talk on stage. We still have a few minutes," Phil said.

"Sounds great," I said.

We went up to Phil's curtained off waiting area
just behind his amp stage right.
The crowd was getting louder.
"From what you sent me already,
your film idea sounds awesome,"
Phil said. "But you might want to wait."

"Why's that?"

"A huge transition is about to occur.
I'm not sure how much time I'll have

in a couple months to work with you."

"What kind of transition?"

"I'm not sure. Just a feeling."

Phil strapped on his bass.

"I felt that way too just before the show. I had a vision."

"What kind of vision?"

"I saw an ocean in the sky and all the sea creatures had moved there."

Phil looked serious. "That's it. That makes sense."

"What's that?"

"Nothing," Phil said. "But I'll have to tell Jerry they got scuba up there. He'll like that."
Phil turned and walked out to the front of his amp.
The crowd was going nuts. He yelled back to me, "Something you want to hear? Don't say St. Stephen!"

"Unbroken Chain!" I yelled back.

"We can do that!"

I stood there behind Phil's amp
and listened to the rest of the show
with laughing baby by my side.
I didn't know what Phil meant about
telling Jerry there was an ocean in the sky,
but not long after that show,
I knew.

ECHOES OF PHIL BY CHANDER DHINGRA

In the amber glow of July's soft light,
Phil's bass lines rose, deep as night,
Like river currents, steady and slow,
Binding hearts in a timeless flow.
Notes hung heavy, yet light as mist,
Each strum, a call, too sweet to resist.
Echoes of days both lost and found,
Where music roamed, unbound, unbound.
The rhythm spoke of mountains high,
Of winding trails beneath open sky,
Each thump a heartbeat, a whisper, a roar,
Of journeys past, of dreams in store.
He played the soul, the pulse, the thread,
Connecting strangers, spirit-led.
In every chord, a life, a tale,
A melody carved on winds that sail.
So here's to Phil, with boundless grace,
A keeper of time, a voice, a place.
In his music's hum, we all belong—
A family bound by Phil's deep song.

LESH PLAYS THE BASS LINE BY JUDE BRIGLEY

I was interested in playing the whole band. From there it got heavier and heavier.

Thanks to his grandmother, music darted
early through his Piscean head. Violin,

trumpet, Berio's avant garde electricity
guided him to composing classes where

in his head he heard all the instruments
together. No accident then that he claimed

the bass to link a harmony to the rhythm
of rock. He dug out the groove,

set the lines, made the Dead complete.
That pizzeria in Menlo Park, didn't know

the half of it, or that this was only
the start of his dark star rising. *Speeding*

 arrow, sharp and narrow, bring
shades and spikes when Lesh plays

the bass line, and picks through
the transitive nightfall of diamonds.

I THOUGHT OF YOU AT SUNRISE BY RENEE CHANDLER

I thought of you at sunrise, Phil
dropping bombs in heavenly domains
All your friends over the years
proud to honor your transition
interdimensional patterns shifting

Training for many years
a seeker of the holy visions
Interpreting waves of thought
in totally unique ways

You shared your soul with us
capturing the intricate dance
between audience and band

You used your rich voice
to harmonize with the boys
amongst a family of angels

Manifesting diversity in sound
that delicately coalesced
with the beating of Mickey's heart
echoing through Billy's chest

Floating through vocals with Bobby
Conjuring solid lines for Jerry to cling to
as he danced among the stars

Mystics, witches, and wizards
dressed in enchanted garments
Hypnotic twirling and singing
slipping through time

Iconic verses transforming the spirit
complete the circuit
uncork the sacred myth

A transcendental orchestra
of psychedelic alchemy
creating a blossoming telepathy

Your incorrigible smile
weaving through ethereal notes
Dazzling, with eyes of love
you welcome us all home
protected and enduring
trips abound

   choir tone

there is an extra twinkle
in your eyes this morning
it is ecstatic energy
exchanging hands and hearts
from this world into the next
we are all balanced
hovering on the lip of a trip
on the hips of uncertainty
darling lotus blossoming

I watched the sunrise this morning
And thought of you, Phil
Drooping bombs in heavenly domains
All your friends over the years
Were there to honor your transition
in and out of the stratosphere
interdimensional patterns shifting

IN MEMORY OF PHIL LESH BY ROBERT COOPERMAN

We caught Phil and Friends one night
not too long after we'd moved to Denver,
at, fittingly, at The Fillmore,
and almost left while the opening act
was making a lot of noise and not much music,
headaches like spiky tendrils of noxious
weeds and Venus flytraps.

Then, thankfully, Phil and Friends,
who played as loud, but actual tunes sweet
as the nectar Monarch Butterflies feast on.

We belted out the lyrics, even if
a tad off-key, everyone holding each other
and dancing to "Tennessee Jed,"
swaying, arm-in-arm to "Ripple"
and "Uncle John's Band.

Oh, that was a long time ago,
and now the news that Phil's gone
to where "A Box of Rain"
can't help him anymore.

He'll be with us on his elegant
electric bass and reedy tenor,
on "Mountains of the Moon,"
singing about Tom Banjo
and the Jade Merchant's Daughter,

and if I believed in such things,
trading licks and riffs with Jerry,
both of them in fine, fine form.

THE ROCK STAR FALLS IN GREATNESS BY MOORE NGWENYA

Your hand was glued to the guitar
strings.
Giving perfect waves of jazz music which
manufactured
the great fame called Grateful Dead .
Which rocked all timelines reaching to
numerous generations.
Taking you to endless concerts as you
grow with greatness.
The rock star falls in greatness.
Conquering all tests of time to the grave.
As the Grateful Dead died to dig out the
Phil Lesh and friends.
Which honoured you in your studio chair.
As you retire not to type the music
Notes.
Heard through the microphone waves
Echoed by the glued hand to the
guitar strings.
As wrinkles tell the tale of your
story
And fame keeps the recordings of
time .
The Rock Star Falls In Greatness

WITH REGARDS BY UZOMAH UGWU

Mad tales play on chords of
Joy and despair, tall trees
Are hit by the wind in four directions
Lettig the wind cover every inch of the words
That beg to say
What songs need to be sung
Made promises with the angels
And the devils to forgive my sins
Heard strong melodies by foreign tongues
Felt your bass line drop below the beats like it knew me well
Where I hope you knew you were missed
Before you were gone and knew you left rain in boxes
That leaves dew as morning comes
Like where it should be heard
So a smile might keep us from the pain
Knowing you won't be coming back for one last song

DEEP, LIKE AN EARTHQUAKE BY PATRICIA J. DORANTES

From every note, a new space.
To create, to live, to freely flow,
You are there, moving with the wind.
A deep sound, that comes from a free soul.
No harm, no sorrow. Only pure freedom.

From every chord, a heartbeat once hummed.
Each strum was a whisper, low and strong,
painting colors in the air, grounding, lifting.
He stood, centered, yet adrift,
a voyager on the currents of sound.

There was no past, no future—only now.
A pulse that bound, a rhythm that breathed.
He would close his eyes, and in that moment,
he was everything, and nothing, at once.

The bass line, his quiet guide,
spoke a language only he knew,
one that resonated deep, deeper still,
reminding him that freedom was here,
in each note that danced through the silence.

LEARNING TO LIVE WITHOUT YOU BY JON LAWRENCE

Do you remember when night clouds
in Saratoga ate the moon like Pac-Man?

When we met Joey, who cut
acid into triangles and pitched

his tent in the pasture? When the
concert was cancelled, but a red-faced

boy, sunburst acoustic on his beer belly
sang just like Jerry, and all the hippies

were spun and were spinning with glow sticks
like the campground was covered in neon crowns?

When a man took that last bump to numb an anger
rising within him, last log on fire,

and we laid on memory foam mats and wondered
if the moon was covered in eggshells, when we know

it's a gritty world up there. Morning
came, each line of smoke trailed from the campsites

like an eraser smudge,
and old Deadhead Paul stuck his phone

to my face and asked
Did you see god in that moon last night?

DEAD HEAD ELEGY BY JIM MURPHY

The time signature was clear but strange.
It wavered, as if the music was bent flame
at the cave's mouth, the chording hands
shadowed in ochre on the walls. Every
nimble footfall sparked the dust with sun-
bright embers. They glowed hot, but faded
fragile inches from the always-twirling blaze.
Whose bones filled all these upset graves?
Whose dreams might still skitter and dance
outside, along electrical currents of air,
striking through the cool Colorado rain?

Written names crack across clay, while
legends float as petals to a whirlpool.
Such is the history of sheer fabrication--
hints of skin under gauze, snapped red
ankle twine and mismatched finger
cymbals--one gaudy tin, one bell-bronze.
What if we never find their partners?
What if the Book of the Dead stays shut,
the record unread, the music unheard,
the companion piece only empty space,
the strings untuned, the harp unstrung?

It's how we mistook our roles in ritual
that buried most of us alive. We didn't
understand how one prismatic note splits
into many, how any word calls forth a world.
If we weren't primed for simple patterns,
we wouldn't have named it *chaos*. If we weren't
so grasping and unsure, we wouldn't have
called the children *lost*. If we weren't so
caught in self, we wouldn't have said *alone*.
We needed a miracle, and ears to hear it
because the times were clear and strange.

AMERICAN ELEGY BY KYMBA NIJUCK

That summer I was 15.
I worked at the flea market.
You played *American Beauty*
Over the loudspeaker
At least once every weekend
Or every day.

It became the soundtrack
To my Saturdays,
Selling designer jeans
That I would never wear,
And Sundays selling bootleg t-shirts
That some stoner dude printed
In the garage of his parents' house
With a meticulously manicured lawn
In the suburbs.

And that music began to permeate
Other days and other places.
You would pick me up
On a Friday night.
Other music would come
Out of the cassettes
And later CDs
From your car's stereo.
But *American Beauty* Was a constant.

We sat in your car
In parking lots Outside stadiums,
The Meadowlands
And the Colosseum
Waiting for the doors
To open,
Listening to our own private concerts
Until they did.

At your memorial
A few years ago

Your nieces told me
They found a Ticket stub
 In your room.
I had had one for the next seat.
Oh, how we danced that night!

THE SECOND GIFT BY WENDY CARTWRIGHT

I saw my first concert when I was 7 – a real rock and roll show!
How could I not be ready for this?

The Grateful Dead at 14. Lawn seats for the five of us: Dad's friend on the and Britany and Jon—two more 14 year olds I convinced the Old Man to bring along. We'd made our way through a sea of matted hair, unshaven ladies, and body odor. I pulled out the glass bead necklaces I had painstakingly threaded to trade them for cigarettes.

Good ole Pops lit each smoke to see if it was laced before I could take the first drag. I guess if I'd have gotten a left-handed one, we'd have spent the night in the car. Dad was the only person who could drive. I'm glad none of them held a surprise.

Somewhere in the middle of a never-ending rendition of "Not Fade Away" that I'm fairly certain is still being played, I felt ole Pops lean and I heard...

"Is Jon down there bummin' hits?"

Panic-stricken, but always thinking fast...
"I don't know, Dad. I'll ask him."

And I did.

Leaning back towards my dad, I relay, "Naw, man, just talkin'."

On the way home, three 14 year olds in the back seat of a two-door whatever—two of us stoned, and one wasn't me—shifted in dazed disbelief with the curves and the experience looking like dominoes that wouldn't quite topple in either direction.

And, two years later, almost immediately after I gave away my virginity, seated on the bed with the radio playing... *Jerry Garcia is dead.*

That was the second awful 16th birthday gift I got that day.

GARCIA'S DEATH BY ROARSHOCK

Yesterday, today and tomorrow
Jerry joined the angels
rounded out his earthly life
left us Dead Heads
sad, but grateful
for all the years
combined.

Lucky! Oh! We are so lucky
who grieve today,
for millions of Dead Heads
yet unborn will never be
in some smokey hall
or out at a country fair
while Jerry and the boys
are playing something
entirely new
and absolutely perfect.

Last week, I hallucinated
(had a premonition of)
a world without Jerry.
I worried, he was gone
without a trace
and only I remembered him.
Turning, I saw an old
Fillmore poster on the wall,
Garcia's youthful, clean-shaven
smiling face
and in my head I heard
his distinctive voice saying
"Don't worry about it, man."

Late Sunday afternoon,
driving home through Forest Knolls
I thought fondly of Jerry.
Two sunrises, three sunsets later,
that's where he died.

Since then, for me
everything is flashback deja vu.
I have already read all the newspapers
and seen all the television programs,
all the galaxies are reruns,
but destiny is just begun.

When the news went round the world
the people took the streets
and danced and sang by candlelight
all across the nation.
I was alone again in my mind's room
and could not share their laughter
or their tears.

Now Jerry rides the cusps
between the times.
The times are changing
as they are encapsulated,
contained on disc and tape,
but even should the poles shift
and all magnets disappear,
erasing Jerry's voice,
even then the songs will be sung
around campfires in the primordial forests
under eternity along the wild
wind swept beaches of nature
inside the castles and caves or bus
where we maintain our freeholds.

Remember Jerry on the stage,
his expressions as the music
played the stories of existence.
Never mind abusive uses
of dangerous substances,
or the impudent impotent reviews
of ignorant imbeciles,
none of that matters.

What matters are the curious

expansive trips further into, out of
spaces and bubbles of consciousness.
Jerry left us many signposts,
and the long strange trip continues
there is much work that remains to be done.

The Grateful Dead can never die
The Grateful Dead are life.

WHAT HAVE THE DEAD MEANT TO YOU? BY DAN O'CONNELL

"We all need a Grateful Dead. I wish I had one." – Jerry Garcia

Nothing.

Everything.

Bodies jockeying / dancing for position

like dust forming a solar system

around a dark star

of which I am not a part.

TRANSFERRED BY M.D. DUNN

That morning, the birds were quiet
The sun through leaves strummed against shadows
sent them rippling across the window
and woke me into a gentle vacuum
like something essential had been released
like creation itself had been renewed
and an answer revealed overnight

I remember the lightness of the day
soft on my body my mind clear of worry
I thought, What great gift is this?
What resistance has ascended?
My roommate still in her robe
shaking watching my face for any grief, said:

Jerry died last night. Jerry's gone.
Without thinking, I wondered out loud
if that is what I had sensed in the stillness.
Maybe that is why I feel so good today,
I said, and she never spoke to me again.

JERRY GARCIA DONE GONE LONG GONE BY BILL NEVINS

So if a certain Boomer-Geezer ever wrote a Slam Poem it might go something like this:

I'm so sick of the Sixties.
Smoky nostalgia's a bore
Teach your children well—Hell!
It's Germany 1934,
so sing me no more
FISH- cheery imagine there's no war songs
(Woodstock was a mud n granola fiddle-fun fest
 while Indochina burned)
Billy Strings doing "War Pigs"
is just about all I can take
now that the Ramones and Strummer
are gone.
I don't want to hear old man Neil sing about
her dead on the ground
when the National Guard is coming 'round
again.
He didn't know her,
and who is she, anyway to him
but a sentimental hook for a hit song
to help with the payments on his ranch?
Young Neil nor Joni never got gassed, shot or beat- up,
and no cop knocked the silver spoon
out of any Canadian folkie's dulcet mouth,
and I don't give a damn about Virgil Kane's
see-shesh brother buried down south.
I don't want to hear Joanie wailing,
"Kumbaya mi lawd"
'cause she thinks Zimmy or her daddy did her wrong
so long, long ago.
Shucks!
She made her bucks.
I don't want to ever again hear Slick Gracie
howl about weatherwoman Diana
building a bomb to kill SDS
while her Starship Plane cruises first class

in comfy Owsley retirement dreams.
I don't want to hear you whine
against being so rich and so outta touch
with the times Watchman Tom and your rusty rage machine
and
Goddesses save us from septuagenarian Springsteen!
and hey Bob your neighborhood bully's
crossed the line, man, for real this time!
How does it feel? To be a pawn in their game?
The Glimmer Twins are now just faded junkies
not street fighting rebels
or sexy dancing monkeys
so
sing us no more vain peace freak battle- songs
as the Empire roars
you dying Nero-dinosaurs.

Get your Tired candy asses in gear
or get your slimy hippy ear-worms outta my ear.
Lou Reed said it best, and Lou is long long gone:
March of the wooden soldiers
All you protest kids:
White Light! White Heat!
I say . . . tin soldiers and Trump and J.D. Vance are coming.
Yer finally on yer own.
Fahgettaboutit! Reetpapareet!
Just play me Martha & the Vandellas doing "Dancing in the Street!"

THE DAY CAPTAIN TRIPS DIED BY M.J. ARCANGELINI
After Frank O'Hara's "The Day Lady Died"

for Jerry

It is 11:20 in California, a Wednesday,
three days after Hiroshima Day, yes,
it is 1995, and I will not get a shoeshine
because I never do. I will get off work in Arcata
at 5:15 and then go to Fields Landing for dinner,
stopping only for a hitchhiker who I won't know.

I walk to the parking lot, muggy sky trying to sun
and eat salami sandwiches while I listen to
world beat radio to hear what the musicians
in Africa are doing these days.

I go to the BLM office
and Keith (first name only on his tag)
issues me a campfire permit while telling me not to build one,
and I get in the truck and drive back to town.
At Northtown Books I buy a copy of Pasolini's *Theorem,*
but before I do I consider maybe getting Anais Nin's *Incest*
diary or perhaps a copy of the Philip Larkin biography or the
large format collection of reproductions of Francis Bacon's paintings
with fold out pages for the triptychs, but in the end I
stick with the Pasolini, and at the last minute grab the last copy of a novel
I remember reading interesting reviews of,

and for Ben I go over to the Co-Op and pick up a copy
of *The Hiker's Hip Pocket Guide To The Humboldt Coast*
and a couple of sun buns for the afternoon and
then I head back across the parking lot to where I came from
the sun heats up the Plaza, and before I climb the
stairs to my office, I see someone wearing a
tie-dyed t-shirt with his face on it,

and I am sweating a lot by now and thinking of
leaning against the side wall at MOJO's,
drunk and passing a joint to the security guard while

he sang his songs and played his guitar for everyone,
and we couldn't stop dancing.

UNCLE JERRY IN OHIO BY HEIDI JOFFE

twenty nine years ago,
he crossed to the other side.

On streets steaming patchouli
and grilled cheese, I mourned

as one of his lost children,
who heard the songs and fled

my home to dance in a troupe
of tricksters, this freak carnival

that passed through town,
on the bus, or off the bus,

my body responds to his thumb
on the strings. Oh, to hear Jerry

again on the banks of the river:
rain falls, and in mud, we spiral.

JERRY GARCIA & GERMAN ROOT BEER BY JOHN DORSEY

for dan harshman

in another life
i sit there drinking
a flat german soda
from a glass bottle
while the two of you
drink from a well
of high school memories
i frame the photo
with a bad poem
thirty years in the past
pimples on my face
the room has gone dark
and; the dead are grateful
just to have been
alive.

DEAR JERRY BY MIKE FOXHALL

Dear Jerry,

I sit here at the end of The Days Between (8/1-8/9) reflecting on a man that has had such an incredible impact on my life who I've only met through his music (and yes, I truly believe that I've met Jerry on a spiritual level multiple times). On 8/9/95, the day we lost Jerry, I was 5 years old living in Montgomery, Alabama. I grew up with Jerry and The Dead's music mainly because of its prominence in pop culture by the time I started listening to music, but I will never forget the first time I really *HEARD* this music.

My art teacher in the fifth or sixth grade was a guy named Mr. Quinn, and to a preteen boy he was the coolest. He was in a band and let us listen to music during class, and one day he turned on the old boombox in the corner and those first 9 notes and first line of the song filled the room "Driving that train/ High on cocaine." The hook was set in that moment. They had a sound I'd never heard before and the rebel child in me loved the balls of telling the world they were high on drugs and didn't care what you thought.

From there I began to find the classics. "Sugar Magnolia," "Touch of Grey," etc. I played around in the casual fan pool for a few years, enjoying their music and discovering bands they had influenced. This is where I began listening to the likes of Phish, Widespread Panic, moe., Allman Brothers, The Band, Dave Matthews, and the like. My taste wandered as I figured out what I liked and didn't, but The Dead remained a stalwart in the rotation.

As college came I dug more into The Dead and began to discover some of the deeper cuts. "Althea," "Sugaree," "St. Stephen," "Shakedown Street," "Estimated Prophet," etc. In conjunction with my deep dive on The Dead I began to dig deeper into one of the bands that really filled the void left by Jerry's death, Phish. These two legendary groups began my journey through the hippy, jam band world we all know and love.

Fast forward to May 29, 2022. I lost one of the most important people in my life to a drug overdose, and I relapsed for the 6th time in as many months. I was lost. I was scared. I felt like I was completely alone. Then one day, with a random Spotify generated playlist playing, it happened. I heard the melody of and Jerry's voice sing "Morning Dew" and I wept. Not because of anything in the lyrics (although they are incredibly beautiful) or the message in the song, but because there is a healing quality to Jerry's music.

Like the good addict I am, I spent days that turned into weeks that turned into months digesting the extensive catalog of live recordings (thank you tapers). It was on in the car, while I worked, and some nights even while I slept. It became the soundtrack of my life, and little by little, piece by piece my shattered soul began to heal. I began to understand Jerry's ethos of peace, love, and music.

But listening wasn't enough, I needed to feel the music flow from my body. So I bought a guitar and started taking lessons. I've gotten to the point where I'm just good enough to know how bad I am, but that's not what matters. What matters is that I get the opportunity connect with this music in a new way and, if I work hard enough, help carry this music to future generations.

On June 20th, 2024, I had the life changing experience of seeing any member of the original lineup perform live. Completely disregarding the amazing venue that is The Sphere, it was the show of a lifetime. Being completely present in the moment, enjoying this music that has influenced, guided, and quite literally healed me, felt like I was touching the face of God. I have been to the mountain top. I have seen the white light. God is real, and God is love, and God is this music.

A piece of me changed that day and ever since I've had this peace in knowing that things are going to work out the way they are supposed to. Life still sucks sometimes, but it's just not as much of a struggle as it used to be. I move through the world with an ease I never knew existed.

Thank you Jerry. That's really all I can say at this point. Without your creativity and vision I don't know where I would be, and quite frankly, I'm glad I never have to find out.

-A Grateful Fan

PIGPEN BY RENEE CHANDLER

As the music spins
In and out of focus
Pig's vocals soar
Dizzy and dark

Yearning way up above
The striated trailing clouds
Floating over the heads
Of dancing kids high on L

Singing and stomping
A soul-bearing blues man
In an improv rock band
The sides of his cowboy hat curled up

His face framed
By ancient dust and tragedy
A melancholic guru
Humble and unassuming

That harmonica tearing at my soul
That deep melodic tramp jive
Pounding out an inferno
Diving into the damned realms

Harmonics and scat
The constant drink in his hand
That golden buzz
Sustaining a halo of sorrow

POETRY IS DEAD BY CORBIN BUFF

Poetry is dead.
God is dead.
The novel is dead.

I walked outside today
For the first time in years
And saw their corpses
Hanging from a fake tree
Made of petrochemicals.

Forklifts littered the background.
Cell towers blinked at me
Beneath the glide paths
Of ever-shrinking airplanes.
Our victory was everywhere.

Among the hum of unseen automobiles,
From out of the fog and smoke of exhaust,
A man appeared in garish orange
And yellow garb streaked with dirt.

"The site is being razed
For a new apartment complex," he said.
"You're not allowed to be here."

Was this our new God?
His voice was like a symphony
Played by the finest extinct musicians,
Composed by hands
That had long rotted into dust.

"It is beautiful," I said.
And he was beautiful too.
I told him so
as the light fled over the hills
And darkness crowded in
On the earth's new job site.

I put my hands upon the tree of corpses
And said a last farewell.

Many hours later, I still smell
Of slow death and gasoline.

"The reek is beautiful," I say.
A reminder of the trade we've made,
The beautiful thing we've built.

HOME WITH THE GRATEFUL DEAD BY CHUCK TAYLOR

Grateful Grateful

Here I'm free from social pain
Dead is the strain and stain
    That's all down the drain

Grateful Grateful

Here I'm dead to their rabid noise
I feel inside this special poise
    I dance the night in praise

Grateful Grateful

Here I'm dead to their hate,
To my former confused state
I'm making my own fate

Grateful Grateful

Here I'm dead to their phony hell
I've broken their idiotic spell
    And am out of their shitty cell

Grateful Grateful

I'm dead to their fucking world
Free from their curses hurled
    With memories now pearled

THE ANSWER IS BY KEN GOODMAN

Consummation meditation
    brainbay to GodSea—
    lets GodSpaciousness relax
    where atoms are empty . . .

What is it that 'lets?'

Direct I AM discovery.

Must it be mysterious?

The answer is thought-free.

BLISS BLISS BLISS BY KEN GOODMAN

Nonfixation on one's senses
isn't stupefied, just no longer
dumbfounded by
        in
        vs. outside; or
post vs. pre—
rested in the most sublime sabbath
activity, mindful of the stable field
atoms are empty . . .
bliss the essence of
bliss self-aware
bliss knows
    thought-free.

LOOK NO FURTHER BY KEN GOODMAN

Emancipated wisdom-eye's
immune to greedy shell.

Oasis in dust desert?

Self-refreshingly skullwell.

*Who can bring one closer to
actual I AM glow?*

Look no further than
unseen/beholder of
      brainbow.

UNCLE JOHN'S BAND BY JUDE BRIGLEY

The tide continues to rise,
but we could be a band,
play our tunes and violins,
Canutes raising a hand.

The crow's no longer talking,
but we know the path to tread.
Fellow travelers follow us,
not grateful and not dead.

For now, the sea is rising,
and faces show their hate.
No longer righteous protest.
Now selfishness is fate.

Uncle John is needed
to speak from beggar's tomb,
as fires rage incessantly
on Facebook, X and Zoom.

But listen to the music
and take your children home,
ignore the voice of venom-
reap what you have sown.

A DREAM WE DREAMED SO LONG AGO BY KEITH FELTON

A fabulous Romana Kandel burned, burned, burned, like meteors of light flaming through wordless skies until there was nothing left but the smell of love, but the taste of love, but the fact of love;
But
Kesey proclaimed, "to hell with facts, we need stories"—and as the story he told goes, the Haight was just a place; the '60s was a spirit; and you're either on the bus or off the bus;
Furthur, a
Wolfe at the Golden Gate chronicled the on-the-bus mystic brotherhood's road tripping down the Day- Glo and the neon of the electric kool-aid high-way of America;
And still furthur,
Didion, reported, that in the place The Haight, anarchy was loosed upon the world and missing children were slouching towards meth mayhem;
But
Thompson observed that in San Francisco "life goes on, hope rises, and love plans for tomorrow;"
But
Brautigan foretold that someday "Time will die, and love will bury it;"
While
The Dead declared it all "a dream we dreamed so long ago."

And yet,
I'm still dreaming.

RIPPLE BY PESACH ROTEM
After "Ripple."

I was walking
on the wooden footbridge
over the marshes
in the Hula Nature Reserve
one late-summer Friday morning
when I looked down and saw a ripple in still water.

I was astonished.
What, I wondered, could it be?
I pondered the question.
It must, I reckoned, be
the spirit of God
moving upon the face of the water.

What else could it be,
here,
in the African-Syrian Riz,
that crack in the Earth
into which the Heavens
pour their secrets,

and now,
in the month of Elul,
when the king is in the field,
and the Divine Presence is accessible
to all who yearn to be touched by it?

I trembled in awe.

And a turtle poked his head up
 from under the water
and grinned.

First published in Nine Mile Art & Literary Magazine, Fall 2018.

RIPPLIN' FOUNTAIN OF YOUTH BY RAYMOND SEWELL
After "Ripple"

The words glow at the Fountain of Youth,
and here I am in total bliss.
I am tickled by lucid colors.
Songs fill the air.

Poetry, love, and lovers shaking the orange trees
and rain falls across America, linking us all,
and the road is always there like a comforting blanket.
I can always cross Turtle Island.
I can always see the bubble that is your hometown, everything.
From a passing highway,
I can rest knowing tomorrow isn't forever.
Reminded we live as body and spirit.

Summer is ending, and I sit on my deck under black tie-dye clouds.
The rain is over the air is still, and my baby, Isla, is leaned against the balcony.
Her dreams cradled by the song "Ripple" on repeat – a Grateful lullaby.
One day she will toss flowers and have babies of her own.
The experience of their music is shared generation to generation. A gentle hand—a soothing melody,
and the words glow, glow, so they did/do.
Wondering where her steps will take our family,
down what roads,
what traditions will matter to her on the traveling wind?

[MY SON AND I SEARCHED FOR] BY DAVID RASKIN

My son and I searched for Urs Fischer's gold-and-silver sculpture in the Fontainebleau casino. It stands 43' tall, and still, we needed three employees to guide us through the Deadheads and Hackers who'd swarmed Las Vegas for their confabs. One guard called it *The Nugget*, but the Title is *Lovers #3*. It resembles two stacked lumps of Play-Doh, and Fischer's thumbprints are big as all hell.
That started me thinking about Bernini's 17th-century marble statue, *Abduction of Proserpina,* and Jeff Koons' chartreuse copy of the Bernini, which decorates the breezeway of a condo development in Florida. These jokes are funny if you're an art history professor, but my kid's a computational biologist: he was more interested in the cracks that snaked upwards from the bottom of the sculpture like a phylogenetic tree. That night, our viewpoints converged as we danced in the Sphere to what remains of the Grateful Dead forty years after I saw my first show. Some 18,000 sang the closing refrain of "Will not fade away." My parents divorced when I was a little older than he is now.

SONGENIZIO ON A LINE FROM "BIRD SONG" BY ANDREW JONES

All I know is something like a bird within her sang
that night by bonfire flicker and johnsongrass sway,
some unknown songstress, braided hair backlit
the orange of a songbird. In that Oregon evening,
the songbook of the Dead opened up to me at last.
For so long I was songless, the magic elusive
despite trying to sing along, despite being born
and rocked in the cradlesong of San Francisco.
To hear those lyrics in plainsong—black throated
and like dew—stirred the sanguine in my sinewy
ligaments and tissues. Don't call it sing-song flirtation;
define it as birdsong magnetite carrying me back
to that sweet song again. A call awakening possibility,
 a song unearthing desire, a voice tempting curiosity.

*The songenizio is an alternative take on the sonnenizio form invented by Kim Addonizio. In this case, the first line is borrowed from a song lyric and one word from that first line is repeated in some form in every one of the following 13 lines with a final rhymed couplet.

TAKING THE T-SHIRT BY KENDALL SNEE

We left dad in New Jersey,
rotting in his prison cell
with his mustache,
and mom's ruined career
to keep him company.

We took with us:
A new criminal record, each,
that would follow us
from state to state/
from job interview/
to buying a car/
to buying a house/
to big relationship leaps...

"If we're going to do this
there's something I probably should tell you..."
& one particularly awkward
D.A.R.E video—
in an 8th grade health class,
where his name would be mic dropped
next to "drug addict" and your classmates would
recognize the man with your name before you do;
because you see so little of him.

We took with us: accidental aiding & abetting
and one black & white
Grateful Dead t-shirt
and got the fuck out of there.

Three jubilant skeletons
played instruments with the cast of
Winnie the Pooh.

Or maybe I'm misremembering.
Maybe I didn't know what a "Dead Bear" was —
so I thought them to be
a bunch of Winnie the Poohs.

Plural. I thought we each could be
one of the skeletons.
One was Dad.
One was Mom.
& I'd be the third.
& I was in the middle
because I wanted to be next to them equally
& they wanted to be next to me.

& we'd play in this imaginary band
that lived on my Mom's T-shirt
& it became the snow globe I dreamt into
of all those Christmases that would never come

& mom would wear that t-shirt like a short dress.
like it was her only piece of clothing,
like she wanted to be buried in it,
like it was her only small rebellion she could afford.
As she collected the pieces
of her life, sheltered in place in
the knowing, but forgiving
"I told you so,"
of her own mother.

Working with kind Principals
who shirked paperwork, hand wrote approvals—
—under the table,
and slowly helped to expunge a record
until we could leave that, too, in New Jersey.

And my mom and me,
we still like the Grateful Dead despite it all.
We always bought into the hippie mantras
and hope for a better world.

And perhaps, that's how we
caught the aiding & abetting charge to begin with,
by being believers
in that one very bad man's bullshit.

And now I don't see the skeletons as my retired family anymore—
no longer touring some blank space canvas for all eternity.
They're just three imaginary friends (& Winnie the pooh)
who watched over me and her as we rebuilt.

But I still like the shirt,
and Casey Jones,
and the Ripple,
and more than anything,
I think being a believer is still a good thing.

CASEY JONES BY KAREN CLINE-TARDIFF

Twice a year for 4 years we met there:
Casey Jones Museum.
Train on display.
Buffet to the side.

It's impossible not to
sing those 4 lines over and over,
and I wonder if you'll be
high this time, pills or
whatever else you use
to numb your existence.

I take my child away from you,
usher him into the cool
air turned humid from steam
tables piled high with mediocre
fried chicken, mushy green beans
and rehydrated potato flakes,

And as you pull out of that
parking lot back onto
the interstate I hum slightly
different lyrics, hoping
your speed catches up
to you, hoping I don't
have to see that train again.

GRATEFUL YOU'RE DEAD BY MADISON GILL-SILVA
for Saint Stinar

1.

I like to think "Peggy-O"
would have played at your wedding.
It would have been you and your mom's
first dance, and she would have thrown
her head back and laughed

not because her name is Peggy,
but at something you said to her
in that close moment with your arms
around each other and your foreheads touching
the rest of us will never know.

2.

I won't ever get to attend your wedding,
but I like to think you were still at mine.

The crack of lightning that lit up the sky
must have started a Fire on the Mountain
somewhere, burning all the way through my vows.

3.

The first time I heard "Brokedown Palace"
was at your funeral. I memorized all the words.
The steal-your-face flower arrangements
were too blue white and red against the dark
wood church. It looked wrong.

As wrong as the little box
they carried you down the aisle in.
Even reduced to ashes, it seemed
like you should have taken up
so much more space.

4.

I bought the tickets and took the pills
at Folsom Field just to feel close to you.

But no matter how hard I squinted,
John Mayer didn't look like Jerry Garcia,

and I couldn't pick your ghost
out of the crowd of writhing bodies,
and their rendition of "Shakedown Street"
was too slow,

and I didn't belong there, and I left early
without even buying a T-shirt.

5.

The night you were released from rehab
I remember our aunt said, *"He'll be an addict
the rest of his life."* Ten years sober
I don't think any of us believed her anymore.

I think we all thought if you were going to die
you would have already. And there you were –
dressed head to toe in tie dye, talking about being a father
to more than just your dogs. Your smile wide
and pupils dilated in every photo at your memorial.

6.

If you were exchanging one
Friend of the Devil for another and
another just to outrun the original demon
that first named you addict –

If every day was a burning room,
you had to smoke more and more
to keep Truckin' through –

If you thought all you had to show
for your life was a trail of broken
Brown Eyed Women and a closet
filled with bones hidden behind hoodies
riddled with cigarette burn holes –

then I understand, you had to go.

7.

I hope you know better now.

8.

And I'm grateful that skeletal fist
is no longer clenched around your throat.

Grateful for the bouquets of Scarlet Begonias
decorating your grave.

Grateful your spirit shed your body
with all its unholy wanting for a vessel that fit
better, which is to say eternity.

Grateful my life was one of the many you touched
and that the fingerprints you left
all over our hearts will Not Fade Away.

TRUE TO ME, TRUE TO MY DYING DAY BY PEGGY BRENNAN
After "Dark Star"

Robert Hunter asked, "What is unclear about that?
I mean, it says what it means."

"Dark Star" encapsulates my relationship with my Higher Power with regards to my sobriety. It is both tenuous and solid as a rock, especially when you consider that a rock is a swirl of molecules.

Gratitude is my medicine. Without it I can't listen to the music play. It can be on, or I could even be creating it (improvisation for the win!), but it doesn't make sense without solid, genuine gratitude. It's taken me years to develop this, yet it could smash to bits in an instant.

So I keep dancing, twirling, trancing, swirling, tripping (now substance free tripping!) and skipping because at any moment it could all be gone and if so, I'd love for the last movement I make to be a lighthearted dance-y skip, and the last words I speak to be "I love you, and thank you!"

The Dead played PeggyO at my first show, when I was 14 and a runaway, on my 2nd trip. They also played the whole Terrapin Suite. (It was Englishtown.) I wasn't a deadhead right away—no, it took quite some time to be recognized, but by now, it's dyed in the wool. Grateful Dead were a user-friendly experience. I will never return to the state of never having experienced that phenomenon no matter what, so I'd like to remain a Wharf Rat and be clean and sober and conscious and serene, during.

Shall we go, you and I?

SATURDAY MORNING AA MEETING AT SAINT BEDE'S CHURCH BY NANCY PATRICE DAVENPORT

the sun streams through the windows
of the church, as sweet-smelling
solstice rain falls softly

Dwayne and I sit,
attentive and serious
cups steaming

we saw rainbows on the way here

I'm still a little distracted

the speaker is a mumbler

and the crow couple outside
have different ideas
of what we should give
our attention to

they scream in the rain gutter
they peck on the window   through   beams
of translucent   light
speckled with sparkling dust motes

and it's just like

any other day that's ever been

life is a celebration

FLYING WITH THE DEAD BY DOUG D'ELIA

Every time I hear a Grateful Dead song
I think of the Doo-dah man.
I never learned his real name
he was just one of those
crazies you meet in wartime.

War moves a soldier in or out,
makes them amphetamine-hyper,
drives them to the edge, death riding, thrill-seeking,
no-holds-barred, don't give a shit commando.
That was the doo-dah man.

When I first saw him, he was hanging
from the chopper door, half in and half out.
One foot on the landing skid, wielding
his M-16 like he was expecting trouble,
or looking for it.

He hit the ground before the
landing skids touched down,
swung his M-16 over his shoulder
and pushed his helmet, decorated with a
Grateful Dead skeleton decal, tight to his head.

"You the Doc deadheading back to Mash?"
Do-dah yelled over the sound of the rotors.
I nodded. I pointed at the row of green body bags,
flies already gathering around the zippers.
"Can you take these six to Graves Registration?"

Some guys are superstitious about
flying with the dead; Do-dah wasn't one of them.
The six green body bags were hardly inside the cabin
when the Huey lifted slowly, floated like a butterfly,
then tilting sharply to one side,

affording me an amusement park ride view
of tall elephant grass swaying under the chopper

like wind-up hula dancers, run amok.
The whole drop took two minutes tops,
and felt more like a drug run than a medevac.

I buckled up, while Doo-dah secured the body bags,
ignoring the hindrance of his monkey harness.
The pilot's handle was written across his black flight helmet,
Cowboy. That much, I would have guessed.
He had a tattoo of his chopper on his left arm.

Doo-dah swung around the cabin,
handle to handle, like Tarzan,
checking this and Tightening that.
I couldn't help thinking that he
was going to fall out of the chopper.

He read the look on my face.
"Relax, I used to work in high steel."
He jumped into the gunner's seat like he was mounting a rodeo bull
and covered his ears with headphones

plugged into a Japanese Akai real-to-real
that was rigged to the bird's electrical system.
His voice bellowed over the rotors; he was singing.
It was St Stephen, a Grateful Dead song. In times
like these, there are not enough saints to go around.

"Saint Stephen with a rose
in and out of the garden he goes.
country garland in the wind and the rain,
wherever he goes, the people all complain
...bucket hanging clear to hell."

It was the first time I had smiled in a while.
 "You a deadhead?" he asked.
I was trying to appreciate the irony
of the situation with dead bodies crowded
around me in various stages of rigor mortis.

Too tired to yell over the noise,
I scribbled a note and passed it to him.
It read, "Fillmore East, 1967.
'St. Stephen' was my first song."
Doo-dah let out a howl.

He continued to speak to me
in the lyrics of the Grateful Dead,
I knew these guys weren't supposed to fly
more than four hours in a day, but looking into
Doo-dah's amphetamine eyes, I would say
    he was pushing twelve.

With a fellow Deadhead on board
 Doo-dah was in his glory,
yelling in my face the entire ride,
15 minutes of machine gun-like tête-à-tête,
mixed with Grateful Dead lyrics as natural
    as a Jerry Garcia guitar riff.

The guys in the body bags had
"Cashed in their chips." Into,
"Once in a while, you get shown the light
in the strangest of places if you look at it right."
His favorite was, "Mr. 'Charlie' told me so."

I quickly gathered my gear when we landed,
anxious to visit the shower tent.
Doo-dah was busy inspecting the chopper
but offered up a, "Keep on Truckin', Doc."
I never saw Doo-dah again.

Back in the World, I looked for him at Dead shows.
I looked for him in the crowd, among the vendors
on Shakedown Street and the Wharf Rat table.
I saw him in the face of every crate pushing,
equipment hoisting, backstage roadie.

Then, on the third night of the Philly shows, I saw him
climbing up a steel girder into the rafters and onto a lighting platform.

He was back in high steel, half on and half off the platform,
waiving his OSHA monkey harness in defiance.
He looked down at me and smiled.

War makes it difficult to anticipate when the ghosts will arrive,
bringing streaking hot jungle visions
seen through eyes dripping with tears and blood,
or are they a reel played on a loop of an Akai stereo,
the sound of the tangling film is the sound of flapping angel wings?

After a while, I stopped looking for Doo-dah.
Maybe he didn't make it back. And I stopped looking
for all the soldiers that I applied a tourniquet to
or stabbed with a morphine syringe. The ones with
physical and emotional scars, living in the basement.
of their Broke Down Palace.

DOO DAH DOO DAH BY DAVID ALEC KNIGHT

And there was Spaced Out Sadie
again man, left behind and hanging
on the corner of Evans and Keith.
And there was Spaced Out Sadie,
my friend, she was snapping her fingers
just like a doo dah man, doo dah man.

And there was Spaced Out Sadie
brother, playing hard on that pavement
playing with her mind's eye marbles.
And there was Spaced Out Sadie
snapping her fingers between her shots
playing her "taw," shooting her shooter.

But all the Aggies rolled away.
And her only Allie overshot.
She only had left one Onion Skin.
And there was Spaced Out Sadie
sister, soon enough bored of her games
asking, "Where's the peoples' lost and found?"

DIRE WOLVES BY DAVID ALEC KNIGHT

An orange moon stares above my cabin,
glares upon the wolves that encircle.
They trespass against me now
as I trespassed against them then,
and now there's nothing left us
to hunt and consume but each other.

I peer from within unyielding, as I fight
a numbness that threatens to overcome:
my tired eyes squint to count their coterie.
It may be a dispassionate trick of moon light
that makes their low snarling expression
look to me a sick and starving smile.

I wonder when does hunger turn to murder,
and are they who surround me now culpable?

I drink the last of my red whiskey,
too fast it goes, no matter how paced,
but it is enough to realize how dire
things are for me within and without.
I play solitaire and lose game after game,
but I could cheat and no one would know.

I go to bed with a knife under my pillow;
my blankets trap no warmth, and dreams dim.
I imagine I am called and wake up insensate,
and when with weak hand I open my door,
a biting wind blows in, shaking hinge and frame,
slamming it open for ravening wolves to follow.

I wonder when does hunger turn to murder,
and are they who surround me now culpable?

THIS POEM IS WRITTEN IN BLOOD BY NANCY PATRICE DAVENPORT

walk a couple of miles
widdershins at dusk

end up at San Francisquito Creek

leave the anchor of technology behind

I can't bear another moment
of social media

trip and fall on soz surfaces
my palms are left smelling sweet

I release myself up to the sky
leave a quarter at the crossroads
sing a song to the nine

the moon rises silent   silver

the albino skunk is around
 somewhere

we are aware of the other

we sit separately   together
a few feet apart
in the *tai chi* grass

listening to the sound of the Grateful Dead
from somebody's Palo Alto bedroom window

Jerry is singing
the crickets are singing
the frogs are singing
the pink moon is singing

saying

>forgive yourself
>forgive yourself
>forgive yourself
>
>forgive yourself
>
>sometimes, courage is simply
>an act of desperation

WhenTheGratefulAngelIsBuried
WhenTheGratefulAngelIsBuried
WhenTheGratefulAngelIsBuried
WhenTheGratefulAngelIsBuried
WhenTheGratefulAngelIsBuried
WhenTheGratefulAngelIsBuried
WhenTheGratefulAngelIsBuried

WORD ART BY MIKE FERGUSON

QUENTIN TARANTINO LOVES THE GRATEFUL DEAD BY TRISH HOPKINSON

But he refuses to admit it. He lies awake at night envisioning
Mountain Girl plucking daisies and braiding them together for a
crown she places on his head. He wakes up late in the day and
writes a screenplay where beautiful women don leather jumpsuits and
slice men in half. He wants you to think he loves a bloody steak
but what he really wants is some lovely agedashi tofu, soft and
drenched in dashi broth and a sprinkling of chopped scallions.

EXT. JAPANESE STEAKHOUSE – HOLLYWOOD

He orders the tofu as an appetizer for his vegetarian friend and
watches wistfully as she slips each delicate piece
between her chopsticks and winces a bit when it's gone, just in
time to cut into his rareness, the blood seething onto his plate,
warm and red. Quentin loves himself some mid-century modern
furniture—the smooth lines, the Eames low-to-the-ground-chairs, the
shag rugs and chrome, but can't risk putting it in his house.

So he hires a designer who stands up a sculpture the shape of a
penis, an oddly placed vase. He falls asleep watching a lava lamp,
the one he bought for a girlfriend on Valentine's Day
and when she left it in the box, and then left him.

Quentin Tarantino loves a good wine spritzer— take a good wine and
add a bit of carbonated water to make it bubbly and not so rich. It
doesn't change the flavor really, just makes it more fun, better
than without— like prosecco, but red and glamorous as his own
blood.
Tarantino loves his own blood. The salty goodness
that leaks from a hangnail pulled. The drip from a scraped knee
after a night of drinking and a poorly placed curb.

EXT. RED LIGHT DISTRICT – SUNRISE

The scabs are even better, crusty and old, hard, like an old man
with lonely eyes. Quentin is lonely, like the old man in his scabs
like the old woman in his pancreas, secreting sweetness
or rather, the lack thereof. He wonders if this witch
writes her screenplays in insulin, if she sucks away the sugar,
if she replaces it with bitterness. He hates the spells she puts on
him,
When she's quiet she's most deadly. Quentin Tarantino hates people
who can't order coffee. It's not that difficult. Why would anyone
walk into a Starbucks without something in mind.

He loves a good cup of coffee. Not a multiple ingredient

mixed mess of caffeine. What he wants is a simple drip poured
into his cup, no pour-over bullshit, no hipster pretentious siphon
or aero press, just your standard Mr. Coffee at a diner
where the server pours it hot and asks if you would like pie.

INT. DINER - MORNING

Mr. Tarantino likes his pie hot and ala mode. Apple is best
but cherry is fine in a pinch. The best vanilla ice cream has bits
of bean and clings to the spoon in an attractive way. He only wants
the waitress to cling to something in an attractive way—bend her
hips across the countertop, her uniform creasing in all the right
places.

He daydreams finding himself in a quiet coffee shop
next to worn out blue-collars and prostitutes.

He wonders if they know more than he does, if they weather
life in a way he can never understand.
He is right to wonder.
Quentin, sweet Quentin, loves dipping his toe in mud
—grit and earth congealing beneath the nail.

It was just last week he had a pedicure, the Vietnamese girl
who scrubbed the bottoms of his feet, giggled a bit when he
flinched, checked her phone while his heels simmered in wax.

The worst part is the grinding on the balls
of his feet. The way she scrapes with reckless abandon.
What if he should remain calloused? He knows the flakes he sheds
are useless. The callouses are beneath the skin.

Tarantino used to give a shit about art
but now he knows he won't get paid for any of it.

SMASHCUT

QT hates driving alone but when he does,
he listens to episodes of My Dad Wrote a Porno.

It's sickly rewarding and funny. He laughs by himself
behind a windshield of splattered bugs and bird shit. He once
found a whole bird stuck in the grill of his Escalade.
He stopped at a convenience store just outside of Las Vegas and
kicked the bird loose with the toe of his tennis shoe.

EXT. SUNDANCE PARKING LOT - WINTER

When the Escalade pulls into Sundance and parks he contemplates moving. It will get cold eventually if he stays in the car, never bothers to step out, never walks to the screening room or to the Owl Bar where someone might ask for an autograph or someone might not.

Mr. Tarantino wears Doc Martins to walk the beach. He doesn't like sand in his toes. He fears the grit.

His pedicurist thinks it's weird. Who wears boots on the beach? But the soles of his feet are soft, smooth as a baby.

Quentin Tarantino wishes he wasn't circumcised.

What if his foreskin cells determined the man he was meant to be. He realizes there are some things he will never know. Like if god is real, does he still have his foreskin? Was he born without one?

INT. QT'S BEDROOM - MIDNIGHT

Tarantino is plagued with insomnia. He often doesn't sleep at all. He watches the numbers flip on his alarm clock and paces a worn space in the wool carpet in the hall.
He used to take Ambien but it made him binge eat and wake up drooling chocolate in the Lay Z Boy with five full-size Snicker bar wrappers at his feet.

He is also plagued with a vicious addiction to nicotine. He's tried it all, Nicorette, Wellbutrin, QuitNet.com, lollipops, the patch, lozenges, spray, inhalers, hypnosis, acupuncture, and laser therapy.

Bottom line is he doesn't want to quit. Although he has quit lots of things. He quit multiple people— girlfriends, toxic family members, booze on occasion, bad boy bullshit, crowds, caring about reviews, caring about awards, caring about what other people think— or not. (He still cares what people think.)

Do they think about his missing foreskin?

Do they know he loves The Grateful Dead?

Maybe he doesn't care if they know.

Quentin likes to have his fortune told. There's not much to tell in the palm of his hand or a Tarot card flipped over, like the numbers on his alarm clock. His future seems certain, death, of course, and just doing what he's always done.

Success will fade, perhaps. But what kind of fortune is that?

EXT. HIGH SCHOOL - SUBURBS

He remembers high school often, not that those were his glory days, but the opposite. He never had the balls to ask out that cheerleader. He'd sit alone at lunch with only his pimples and greasy bangs to keep him company.

Even the other nerds and drama kids ignored him. You'd think there'd be some retribution in the fame he's garnered. There's not.

Quentin always wanted to be a stunt man, wanted the thrill of throwing himself through sugar glass, falling from the 32nd floor, driving a pickup truck off a cliff, wearing a fire suit and careening into a crowd. It's too late for that kind of self-indulgence.

Plus, he was always afraid of being in the background. Maybe he can be the stunt man after all.

INT. FALSE BACKGROUND HANGS IN LOBE 1;
LOBE 2 SPORTS A GREEN SCREEN

The brain is a terrifying thing to let wander. But his imagination is a scab just waiting to be picked. He flicks the dried, dead crust and watches as the red rises to the skin, lets the drop coat and pool before hanging itself in a quiet, slow trickle.

CUT TO BLACK.

First publication in Drunk Monkeys

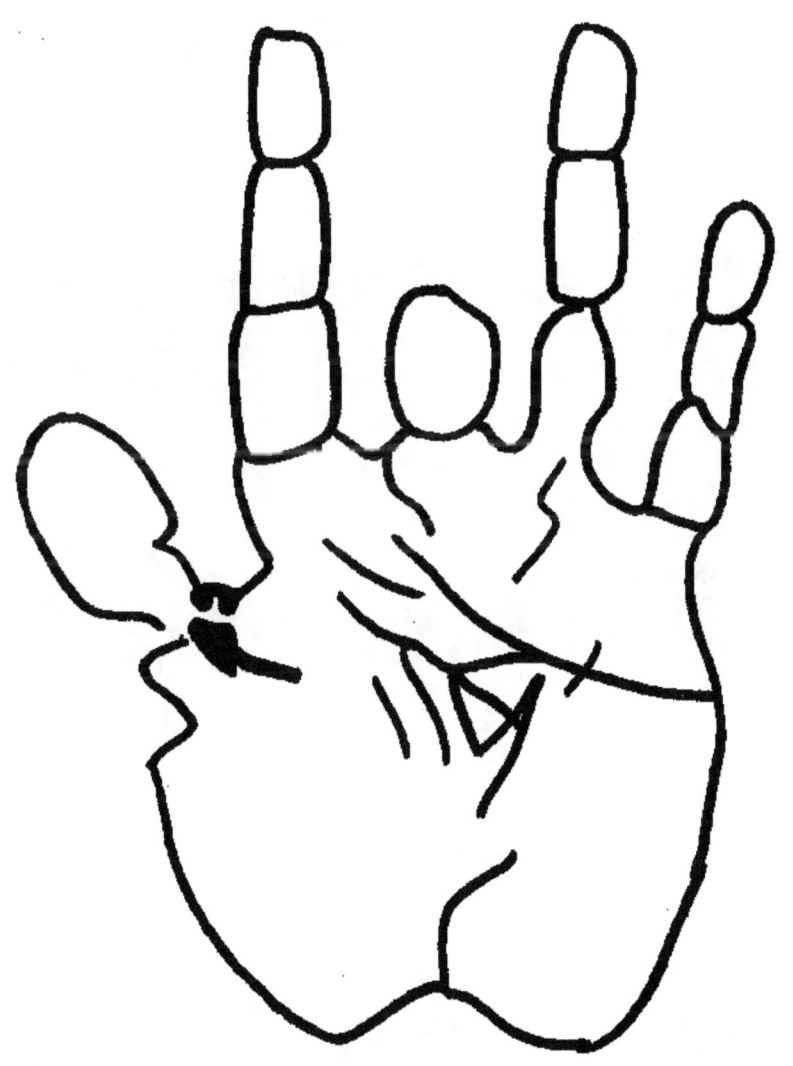

ALSO FROM HERCULES PUBLISHING...

The Original

POETRY IS DEAD: An Inclusive Anthology of Deadhead Poetry

Available from Amazon, or ask for it from your favorite Indie bookseller

www.ingramcontent.com/pod-product-compliance
Lightning Source LLC
Chambersburg PA
CBHW070824250426
43671CB00036B/2055